OF

CURING, PICKLING, AND SMOKING

MEAT AND FISH,

BOTH IN

The British and Foreign Modes;

WITH

MANY USEFUL MISCELLANEOUS RECEIPTS,

AND FULL DIRECTIONS FOR THE CONSTRUCTION OF

AN ECONOMICAL DRYING-CHIMNEY AND APPARATUS,

ON AN ENTIRELY ORIGINAL PLAN.

BY

JAMES ROBINSON,

EIGHTEEN YEARS A PRACTICAL CURER.

British Library Cataloguing-in-Publication Data
A catalogue record for this book is available from the
British Library

Preserving and Canning Food: Meat Curing

Food preservation has permeated every culture, at nearly every moment in history. To survive in an often hostile and confusing world, ancient man was forced to harness nature. In cold climates he froze foods on the ice, and in tropical areas, he dried them in the sun. Today, methods of preserving food commonly involve preventing the growth of bacteria, fungi (such as yeasts), and other micro-organisms, as well as retarding the oxidation of fats that cause rancidity. The earliest curing consisted of nothing more than dehydration; early cultures utilised salt to help dessicate foods, and this was a well-known technique almost everywhere on the globe. Food curing dates back to ancient times, both in the form of smoked meat and as salt-cured meat. The Plains Indians hung their meat at the top of their teepees to increase the amount of smoke and air coming into contact with the food. Drying, essentially reduces the water content sufficiently to prevent bacterial growth, and salt (or sometimes sugar can be used) draws the moisture from the meat via a process of osmosis. In the 1800s, and before, chefs and lay-people alike experimented with different sources of salt (rock salt, sea salt, spiced salt etc.) and it was discovered that certain types of salt gave meat a red colour, instead of the usual, and somewhat unappetising grey. The active ingredients in this type of salt would have been either nitrates or nitrites, and they also helped inhibit the growth of

Clostridium botulinum; a toxic bacteria often found in old meats. In the new age of consumerism, this technique was soon picked up by butchers and storekeepers alike to appeal an increasingly prosperous population. This salt, often coloured pink to differentiate it from table salt, is now used in cured meat production on a massive scale. Sea salt added to raw ham to make Prosciutto, has became one of the best known, and most expensive exports of central and northern Italy. Today, we do not simply cure and preserve out of necessity, but because we enjoy it.

PREFACE.

In laying this book before the public I lay no claim to personal merit, having originally received much useful information from intelligent foreigners, and such of my own countrymen as had repeatedly visited the European Continent. I have, however, been at the trouble and expense of making frequent trials in various processes, and have been favoured by the approbation of many persons in the higher grades of society, whom I have every reason to consider competent to decide upon the quality of my productions.

Englishmen, in general, are distinguished for the great satisfaction they

have in setting before their guests any
thing that is rare or excellent of its kind;
and, since our own markets present the
finest-fed meats and fish in abundance,
why should we doubt of obtaining in our
own homes, many or all the rarities for
which we have hitherto been obliged, and
at great expense, to have recourse to other
countries ?

I beg, respectfully, to draw the atten-
tion of the country squire, the retired
gentleman, and the public generally, to
the following pages, with the assurance
that, if the directions therein contained be
strictly observed, the articles will not fail
to reward the labour and trifling expense
bestowed in their production.

To the fishmonger this treatise may
prove valuable, as, in numerous cases,
redundant stock may be put into pickle,

and thereby be saved until he is at leisure to complete the process; thus avoiding the expense of getting cured goods from a distance, as well as being able to insure the quality.

In conclusion, I may state that I shall, at all times, be infinitely obliged by any suggestions that may tend to enlarge and improve these few pages.

THE AUTHOR.

CONTENTS.

THE

WHOLE ART

OF

CURING, PICKLING, AND SMOKING.

THE SMOKING-CHIMNEY AND APPARATUS.

A SMOKING-CHIMNEY of the following description and dimensions may be erected at a very trifling expense, and will be found quite sufficient for ordinary purposes. It should be placed in some outhouse or shed, or even in a yard, so that no annoyance may be caused to the inmates of the dwelling, by even the smallest escape of smoke. It should be built of brick, and carried up to the height of eight feet at least from a brick or stone floor, one yard wide

B

and two feet deep inside measure, and at the height of three feet from the floor there should be a door frame reaching to the top of the chimney, or nearly so, on which a door, well jointed and fitted, must be hung. A small door of a foot and a half square, of sheet iron, must also be made on the floor, through which the embers from the fire may be raked, and fuel or sawdust added from time to time, as the process of smoking goes on. A false floor, of sheet iron, perforated all over with holes, three quarters of an inch in diameter and four inches apart, must be placed (not fixed) inside the brickwork, on a level with the bottom of the wooden door-frame, viz. three feet from the floor; this will serve to scatter the smoke equally in its ascent,—be a preventive to danger from flame, if any should arise, — and receive any small fish that may fall off the frames on which they are suspended. Four strong iron rods, with moveable hooks on them, must be inserted in the brickwork near the top of the chimney, from which may be suspended sides of bacon, hams, heavy salmon, &c. &c. An outlet for the smoke must be made at or near the top, and a wooden pipe, four inches square, with a slide or valve in it (to confine or dismiss the smoke at pleasure), will completely rid the premises of any unpleasant odour. On each side of the chimney inside, and above the false floor, a frame-work of inch-square scantling must be fixed, with bars of wood of the same size nailed across to rest the rods and frames on; the bars must be fixed eleven inches above each other, and be continued until they come to the iron rods.

The wooden rods or spits on which herrings are to be hung should be perfectly round, one yard in length, from half to three quarters of an inch in diameter, and pointed a little at one end that they may more easily be run through the gills of the fish. They may be of deal or any other tough wood, and sixteen herrings will smoke conveniently on each rod.

Frames for sprats and other small fish must be made thus: — The rims or outsides may be of deal, three-quarters of an inch thick, and two inches wide: the whole frame must be one yard high, and two feet nine inches wide, that it may fit into the chimney without trouble; and on each end of the top bar must be screwed a small plate of thin iron, projecting beyond the side of the frame one inch, which will serve to hang the frames upon with the bars that are fixed up the sides of the chimney. Then take small deal rods half an inch square, and with a brad-awl or sprig-bit insert thirty-two sprigs, at equal distances from each other, in each rod, which, of course, will be two feet nine inches long; and if the sprigs be driven through on each side, it will be seen that each rod will carry at this rate sixty-four fish. These must be nailed on to the outside frame at the distance of four inches and a half from each other, and consequently each frame, when completed, will have eight bars holding sixty-four fish each, or five hundred and twelve on each frame. Wrought-iron sprigs may be used, which (being more than an inch long, and driven up to the head) will project half an inch on the other side, and thus serve to hang small fish on; but this is left to the choice of the party making the frames; and if they are driven in with the points directed upwards, it will be easy to loosen the fish, when smoked, from the nails by turning the frames upside down, and shaking them over a sheet laid on the floor.

A horse or frame of wood of two inches square scantling, with ribs one inch square nailed across the sides, and eleven inches apart, will be requisite to hang the herring rods on, along with the frames, when they are drawn from the chimney ; and for the purpose of cooling the fish, it should be placed in a draught of air. Mackerel, or any other fish that will not suit the frames so well, may easily be suspended from the herring rods by small wire hooks made to run on them.

The draught of smoke in the chimney may be increased or diminished at any time by opening more widely the iron door at the bottom; and if you want to inspect the articles while they are smoking, you may smother the smoke entirely for a few minutes by scattering sufficient sawdust over the embers: only take care that the sawdust is perfectly dry before attempting to use it.

In putting the rods and frames into the chimney, be careful that the fish do not touch each other, but rather place them so that a free current of smoke may ascend between them; for instance, three inches apart. As to fuel, the fire may be lighted with shavings and chips of deal; but oak sawdust should be used generally, mixed sometimes with beech, birch, and other woods. I decidedly prefer the small branches of the oak, such as charcoal is made from, after it has been peeled for the tanner's bark: for these emit a much milder smoke than the sawdust of adult wood. They should be procured in the proper season, and stored in a dry room or shed. Never use old oak or other slabs (which are often little more than sap), nor old barrels, not knowing what

their contents have been. I have known fish
and meats that have been excellently cured
utterly spoiled in the ,smoking. As a general rule I would direct, that, when delicate
articles are to be smoked you should make use
of the milder woods, and dust mixed with oak;
but for hams, bloaters, &c. the stronger flavour
is the best. The embers must never be disturbed while any goods are smoking, as dust
would ascend and spoil their appearance.

BLOATERS.

If the quantity of herrings to be cured will
admit of it, the very small ones should first be
picked out and put aside for making Dutch herrings, particularly if they are rich, fat fish, such
as the Manx in July and August. Next divide
the largest you can find from the bulk; you will
then have two sizes to be smoked. Take common
salt, as rough as you can get it, and with soft
or pipe water make a pickle sufficiently strong

to float an egg, so as to show its surface to
the size of a shilling. Then immerse the fish,
keeping the two sizes separate, by means of
boards placed on the top of them, completely
covering and pressing them down with pieces of
flag-stone, bricks being porous and apt to get
foul. At the expiration of eight hours from
the time of immersion take out the smaller
fish, and stick them on the rods through one
gill and out at the mouth; hang each rod on
the drying horse, and there separate the fish,
leaving them equidistant from each other; in
four hours more treat the larger fish in a similar
manner, and, after they have all dripped well,
put them into the chimney to be smoked, and
pour away the pickle, which would otherwise
become offensive, and spoil your tubs or vats,
which should be well cleansed and set to dry.
Close the door on the fish, and, if requisite,
paste strong paper where it fits in the door-
frame, and make a small fire of shavings, which
will dry the surface of the herrings for half
an hour, after which you will get a thorough

smoke on them by putting sawdust from oak, without mixture of any other woods, round your fire on all sides, and a small quantity on the top, and replace it as it is consumed. Continue this process until the fish have acquired the colour you wish, and generally fifteen hours will bring them to a light or London shade; but if you want them of a bright golden colour, they may remain five or six hours longer, though much depends upon the strength of your smoke. Preparatory to drawing them, cover the fire at the bottom with sawdust completely, and in ten minutes proceed to take them out, and then put them to cool on the horses for twelve hours at least. They will be safer remaining thus suspended, but if wanted for packing: take them off the rods at the end that is not pointed, and avoid breaking the gills.

Let me remark that if the herrings come from a distance, and partly salted, it will be requisite to wash off the salt, and any filth that may have attached, before you put them into pickle. And lest you should run any risk of making them too salt, in consequence of not knowing how long they had been in salt before you got them, it will be well to cook one, as soon as they become stiff in the pickle, to ascertain, by the taste, how much longer they will require to remain in it. If they are to be packed for sending away, it will be best done by placing them back downwards, and very close together, excluding the air as much as possible.

DUTCH SALMON.

Select a perfectly fresh salmon of fourteen pounds, or thereabouts, short and thick, with a small head. Wipe the outside quite clean with a cloth dipped in salt and water and squeezed dry, and place it on a firm table, with the back close to the edge thereof, and consequently towards you, and commence splitting it at the head with a sharp strong knife, the blade of which should be about six or seven inches

long, which you must pass steadily and regu-
larly down above the back bone and back fin
(yet so immediately upon them that they may
be left quite bare) to the tail. Lay open the
fish, then, quite flat on the table, take out the
inside, the gills, and eyes, and wipe the cavities
quite clean. Commence taking the back bone
out at the head with a strong-bladed penknife,
which must be run down it on one side until
within six inches of the tail, and no farther, and
then turning the fish, do the same on the other
side of the bone, and it will come out neatly :
that part of the bone which remains unmolested
at the tail will serve to strengthen the fish when
it comes to be hung up. Next, the thick side
must be made to look as though no bone had
ever been there, which will be effected by
flattening down the sides of the cavity, and
paring them in a small degree; but pressure with
a broad flat knife will accomplish it in general.
When the fish is brought into handsome form,
and is quite clean, take fine table salt, and make
a bed of it to suit exactly the form of the fish,

and cause it to be highest in the middle, that
when the salmon is laid upon it the belly may
then be on a level with the thick side. Strew
bay leaves (having previously picked the stalks
out) plentifully upon the salt, and place the
scale side firmly down upon it, supporting the
edges well, and, putting more bay leaves on the
fish, cover all over with salt to the thickness of
an inch, then place a board flat upon it, and
put heavy weights on it. When it has lain in
this way thirty hours, place it flat on its red
side on the table, and put three thin laths of
wood with pointed ends across the back to keep
it extended; the incisions to receive the ends of
the laths should not extend below the skin, if
possible. Then put the fish in a tub of pure
water, and brush off the salt nicely, and hang
it up (by a strong string tied closely round the
tail and close up to the bone) to drip for six
hours at least, after which put it in your chimney, suspended from one of the iron bars, and
dry it there three hours with a warm smoke,
and subsequently with a thorough fume until

it becomes a bright red colour, which may take perhaps thirty-six hours; then take it out and hang it on the horse to cool, and the next day the colour will come up, and it will be fit for use.

In cutting the fish into slices for broiling, the knife must be laid obliquely across it, by which means the pieces will come off much broader than if cut in the usual way. Of all modes of curing salmon, this seems to give the most general satisfaction; and it will be seen that a necessity exists for taking out the bone, in order that slices may be cut at pleasure without mutilating the remainder of the fish.

DUTCH HERRINGS.

Having selected the smallest herrings, take out the gills and gut as neatly as possible at the head without removing the roes, and wash them thoroughly in strong salt and water at least three times; dry them with a cloth, and lay them in an earthen pan, or perfectly sweet tub, out of which the head has been recently taken, and pour over them the following pickle : —

Water that has been boiled and become cold				1 gallon
Common salt	-	-	-	2 lb.
Bay salt	-	-	-	1½ lb.
Sal-prunelle	-	-	-	3 oz.
Saltpetre	-	-	-	2 oz.

If the herrings are fat (for which they would be preferred) there will, in a fortnight, arise on the top a yellow froth or scum, which must be taken off until none appears, as it would, by exposure to the air, in time become rancid. Fill up the vessel from time to time with more fish, and keep them always well covered with the pickle by laying a piece or pieces of clean slate on the top of them (wood might impart a bad taste). When you wish to pack them in jars, or small kegs, take care that they are filled up to the bung or head. These will be more mellow and better in six months, yet they may be eaten in three weeks, or so, if required, and should be treated thus: take out a fish, and, without wiping or washing it, take off the skin, cut the fish across in pieces, half an inch in breadth, and pour a spoonful of the pickle over it. Dry toast, or bread and butter, should be sent to table with them. But I have seen them introduced with wine, particularly where the party has sat late.

SMOKED SPRATS.

As fresh sprats generally come to hand as they issued from the nets, it will be necessary to pick out the largest, and then the second size, rejecting the remainder, or refuse, which, however, may be useful to pot. Your fish being kept separate, must be put into baskets, and well washed in salt and water, then set to drain an hour, and afterwards plunged into a pickle that will float an egg, as for bloaters (see page 7.): the smaller ones may be taken out of pickle in four hours, and the large ones in six hours, and be set to drain; which done, proceed to stick them on your frames, the eye

being pierced by each nail, and then, with a
steady hand, put into the chimney. Set on a
gentle heat for half an hour, and let it be succeeded by a strong smoke for twelve hours
longer, and you will find them of a bright gold
colour, and they will then be " Bloated Sprats,"
and when cold will be fit for immediate con-
sumption; but if you want them to keep a
month or so, you must continue the smoke on
them for thirty hours, or until they become a dark
brown colour; and if for packing, they should
be placed as bloaters, keeping the same-sized
ones together in a dry room, and after a few
hours they will have sweated in the packages,
and will be very mellow and fine flavoured.

SMOKED MACKEREL.

Take the mackerel as soon as you get them,
(for they quickly become dark and lose flavour,)
and with a light knife split open the back from
head to tail; take out the guts, roes, and livers,
(save the two last if you are making Caveach

mackerel at the same time,) also the gills, and be particular you do not burst the gall. Wipe each fish well inside and out, and put them into the following pickle: —

Cold pure water -	-	-	- 1 gallon.
Saltpetre	-	-	- 1 oz.
Common salt	-	-	- 2 lb.
Coarse sugar	-	-	- 1 lb.

If the fish be large and thick, let them lie in this state six hours, then take them out and put two stretch laths across the back of each, extending them as much as possible; wash them through the pickle once, and hang them to dry for two hours; after which place them in a hot smoke for one hour, and afterwards in a cool one for twenty hours, or until they become of a dark-bright chestnut colour. When cold, pack them one on the other in bundles of six, and keep them rather in a dry than in a damp room. These are much esteemed, particularly on the Continent, and by mariners. In Germany they are called May fish, from the fact of mackerel being in high season in that month.

c

DRIED WHITINGS.

These tender and delicate fish soon lose their flavour; and as they are frequently taken in great abundance, and are consequently cheap, they may be cured with considerable advantage. Split them open at the belly from the head to just below the vent, and, after cleaning them out, place them in fine salt for six hours, then wash them in salt and water, and hang them up to drip for two or three hours. They will not require stretching open since the back is not split like haddocks; but white pepper must be rubbed well inside of them to prevent flies from settling while they are hanging in the sunshine to dry, or in a warm room. You may smoke them four hours if you choose, which will effectually preserve them.

KIPPERED HADDOCKS.

In the absence of Finnon Haddies, you may take some fresh ones and split them open at the belly, cleaning them well with salt and water, and taking off the heads. Then lay them com-

pletely open leaving the back bone in sight, and
put them into the following pickle: —

Soft water	-	-	-	- 1 gallon.
Brown sugar	-	-	-	- ½ lb.
Saltpetre	-	-	-	- 1 oz.
Common salt	-	-	•	- 1 lb.
Bay salt	-	-	-	- 1 lb.

If the fish are large, let them remain in pickle
six hours, then take them out, and let them
drip from the frames for three hours, then put
them into the chimney, and smoke them well
for twelve or fourteen hours longer. If you
have any dried fern at hand, it may be buried
in the sawdust when you add to the fire, but do
not allow it to blaze away, or it will be of no
effect.

SMOKED EELS.

Eels for smoking should not weigh less than
half a pound each. Cut off the heads, fins, and
tails, lay open the bellies from the head to the
vent, and clean them out very nicely, not
breaking the galls. Then take small wire

skewers, and form each fish like a figure 8 therewith. Immerse them in salt and water four
hours; take them out; and when dripped, rub
cayenne pepper and mace, beaten finely, inside
of them, and sew up the belly for three inches
only, just in the middle. Smoke them twelve
or fourteen hours, and when wanted, broil them
over a slow, clear fire, until the fat begins to
escape. But I should recommend a fine eel of
from two to three pounds to be skinned, the
head, &c. to be cut off, and split entirely open,
laying the bone bare, which should be taken
out thoroughly and neatly, as well as any of
the lateral ones that come in sight. Then lay
it in salt and water, strong pickle, six hours;
take it out, dry it well with a clean cloth, and
rub in the following paste, just as much as will
cover it all over to the thickness of a six-
pence : —

One large anchovy, beaten well in a mortar.

Bay salt -	-	·	-	- 1 oz.
Brown sugar	-	-	-	- $\frac{1}{2}$ lb.
Saltpetre -	-	-	-	- 1 oz.

Sweet lard sufficient to make all into a paste.

This done, roll up the fish, beginning with

the tail, as tightly as you possibly can, and
bind it with a tape; next sew it up in a
cloth, leaving the ends bare; put it into the
chimney, and let it remain there five or six days
in a strong smoke; and after it has got perfectly cold and firm, in two days more you may
cut off a slice or two, which should be broiled
over a clear fire, and will be remarkably fine.
It will keep twelve months in a dry cupboard,
and improve greatly.

SPRATS AS ANCHOVIES.

Many have been the attempts to make anchovies from sprats; but those who are well
acquainted with each species, and have compared
them, will say decidedly that it is impracticable,
so different are they in shape, flavour, and quality. Perhaps I may be permitted to state that I
have succeeded better than the generality of ex-
perimentalists in assimilating them, but there are
insurmountable difficulties which I leave others
to contend with. I have indeed produced a

highly palatable and useful substitute for the anchovy, in seasons when that fishery has proved a failure, and they have been at a high price in consequence. It was done as follows:—

Take a peck of fine fresh sprats, pick out the small ones and refuse carefully, and without either washing or wiping, put them into a wide jar without a neck, having previously taken the heads off and drawn the gut, and scatter between each layer the following mixture:—

Common coarse salt	- 1 lb.	
Saltpetre - -	- 2 oz.	
Bay salt - -	- 1 lb.	all beaten fine.
Sal-prunelle - -	- 2 oz.	
Cochineal, powdered finely 2 oz.		

Let them be pounded *separately*, and mixed with great care, and *thoroughly*. Fill the jar up to the top after you have repeatedly pressed down the contents, and cover them with bay-salt, and then tie bladder or leather over all. In three months you must take distilled water, one quart, in which you will dissolve a penny-worth of bright red bole armeniac, and grind it until no sediment remain; you may then, but not till then, pour it over the sprats; and when it has saturated the fish and reached the bottom, turn the jar upside down, having secured the mouth, and so on every day for a week; after this they will be fit for use, but always keep the fish covered with the damp salt.

SMOKED ANCHOVIES

Are much in request by epicures, and would be greatly esteemed by others, but they are rarely to be met with, even in the metropolis, and are, consequently, expensive; and since no connoisseur in wine should be without them, I subjoin the information requisite to obtain them. The process is tedious; but with care and patience we shall succeed in procuring them at the most moderate rate.

If on purchasing a barrel of anchovies or Sardinias, you find that they are dry and clotted together, or in the trade phraseology, have not been fed, pour the following liquor gently all over the top layer of fish, without disturbing the salt which covers it : —

> Water boiled and become cold 1 pint.
> Gum dragon 1 oz. ⎫
> Saltpetre -   1 oz. ⎭ dissolved totally.

Let it soak through the fish to the bottom of the barrel, and pour it back again into a basin, then pour it over them again and again, until you can take out the fish singly without breaking them. Get the rough salt off them with a fine brush, hang them on the nails of your frames, and set them to smoke with a very moderate heat and powerful fume, until they have a bright brown appearance, and when quite cold take them off singly, and place them carefully in a new cigar box which you have lined with paper on purpose.

SMOKED PILCHARDS AS SARDINIAS.

Thirty years since, smoked Sardinias might be bought in Billingsgate market occasionally, and were deservedly esteemed ; but subsequently the supply diminished, and none have been recently seen for sale.   I could never account for this, nor did I ever meet any one in the trade who could give a good reason for their disappearance.   The following will be the means of providing a good substitute for them : — Take a peck of fine fresh pilchards, pull off the heads, and take out the gut neatly and thoroughly.   Wipe them well, but do not wash them ; and having placed them closely down in an earthen pan or perfectly sweet keg, scatter the following mixture (the ingredients being well blended) between each layer : —

Bay salt	-	-	- 2 lbs.
Cochineal, beaten fine	-	-	- 2 oz.
Bole armeniac	-	-	- 2 oz.
Sal-prunelle	-	-	- 1 oz.
Saltpetre	-	-	- 2 oz.

Press them down, and having covered them well over with bay salt, put a heavy weight on the top, and a week afterwards pour over them a pint of good anchovy pickle, and let them remain one month at least.   Then take them out, brush off the salt, and hang them on the frames (without wiping them) to dry six hours; after which, smoke them for forty-eight hours, or until they become a dark-brown colour, and, when quite cold, lay them in cigar boxes that have never been used before.

PILCHARDS AND SPRATS IN BUTTER.

For this purpose the fish must be quite fresh, or I would not recommend the trial. Take fine large sprats in December or January, after which they begin to lose their fatness and flavour; or pilchards, when in the height of their season. Take off the heads, and clean them well by opening them at the belly, and rinsing them three times at least in salt and water, making fresh each washing, and dry them well with cloths; then lay them in a pan, with the following pickle poured over them for two hours (not longer) : —

Bay leaves, finely cut - -	- 1 handful.
Common salt - - -	- $\frac{1}{2}$ lb.

White pepper	-	-	- - 1 oz.
Water -	-	-	- - 1 quart.

These must simmer together for one hour, and must be cold when used. Take the fish out, dry them between clean cloths, and lay them out to harden on a table in a warm room two hours longer, then take

Fresh butter	-	-	- - 1 lb.
Mace (beaten fine)	-	-	- 1 oz.
Bay leaves	-	-	- 1 handful.
Fine salt	-	-	- 2 oz.

Let this mixture simmer (not boil) one hour, and strain it through a sieve; put it back into the saucepan, and dip each fish, while the butter is warm, into it, and lay them in oval pots as closely as possible, and press them down well; when cold, pour clarified butter over them, and they will be excellent when brought to table.

SMOKED LABRADOR SALMON.

Labrador fish, though perhaps the finest in the world when fresh, comes to us in salt, and

if wanted in a smoked state must be dealt with
as follows : —

Immerse the fish in soft cold water for forty-
eight hours, if above six or eight pounds each,
changing the water three times at least; then
with a middling hard brush and warm water
clean the outside well, particularly about the
fins and tail; turn it over on its back, and take
off with the brush, and sharp knife, all the skin
and small gut which may have escaped the
notice of those who salted it. Take out the
gills very neatly, and brush the whole face side
until it becomes perfectly clean and red,
scouring the bone until no scurf comes up.
Next take out the back-bone as neatly as
you can, as in the Dutch salmon, and press and
pare the fish into shape. Suspend it by the
tail in a barrel of clean cold water for twelve
hours more, and hang it up to drip for six
hours, and laying it on a clean table, introduce
three stretching sticks into the back, having
previously wiped the scales and fins quite dry.
Hang it up in the chimney with a smart heat

for two hours, and then put on a strong smoke, in which you may keep the fish for twenty-four or thirty hours, or until it has become of a dark red colour. Cool it twelve hours, and cut it obliquely across like the Dutch salmon.

COD SOUNDS.

Take out the sounds carefully with a knife, and wash them well in salt and water; dry them between two cloths, and hang them to dry on your frames for six or eight hours; then get coarse common salt and saltpetre beaten finely, with bay salt, and put this between each layer of fish as you may get them, taking care always that they be not exposed to the air. Many persons throw the sounds away in ignorance, though in the higher classes of society they are much esteemed.

PICKLED SMELTS.

(PREFERABLE TO ANCHOVIES.)

Gut and wash your smelts very clean, and lay them in rows on their sides in a stone jar, and scatter between each row the following : —

Pepper - - - -	- 1 oz.
Mace - - - -	- $\frac{1}{2}$ oz.
Cloves - - - -	- $\frac{1}{2}$ oz.
Salt - - - -	- $\frac{1}{2}$ lb.
Saltpetre - - -	- 1 oz.
Cochineal, finely powdered -	- 1 oz.

These must be well mixed. Then boil as much of the best red-wine vinegar, as will cover them completely, and, when cold, pour it over them, and tie all close with a bladder.

MIRAMICHI HERRINGS.

The winter months, when fresh herrings come shot or without roes, is the season to cure them in this way, and many persons are loud in their praises of them.

Wash the fish well in strong salt and water, and next put them in a strong pickle for twenty-four hours; then take them out, put them on the rods, and smoke them six hours, after which wipe each fish with a linen cloth that is wet with spirits of turpentine, as they hang on the rods, and smoke them until they become of a bright dark-brown colour. When cold, and perfectly firm, put them into a clean calico bag, sew it up at the mouth, and let them lie a month in new sawdust of pitch pine; they will then be fit for use.

KIPPERED HERRINGS.

Split open the fish at the back with a small knife, take out the roes and guts, and put them into pickle as for bloaters, and after you think they are salted enough, hang them on the sprat-frames to drip; then on a clean table, with their backs upwards, put two stretchers across each fish, and again suspend them on the frames, and smoke them until the backs are of a bright

yellow tinge. They are preferred thus, as being
quite ready for broiling or toasting; but the roe
is lost.

BUCKLAND SPLIT HERRINGS.

This preparation of the herring is now seldom
met with, but was greatly in vogue some years
since.   In the summer, when they are fine and
rich, take herrings, wash them well in pickle,
split them open at the back, take out the gut
and gills, and wipe them out quite clean with
cloths.   Place stretch-sticks across the backs,
and put them in the following pickle of

Strong common gin - -	- 1 pint.
Water - - - -	- 1 pint.
Cloves, beaten to powder -	- 2 oz.
Mace - - - -	- 1 oz.
Bay Salt - - -	- $\frac{1}{4}$ lb.
Saltpetre - - -	- 1 oz.

After lying eight hours in pickle, take them
out and hang them up to drip, after which
smoke them until the face side becomes a brown

or chestnut colour, and, when cold, pack them in bundles of six each, and keep them in a dry place.

POTTED SALMON.

As formerly practised at Newcastle.

Take a salmon, split it at the back and through the belly, making two separate sides of it. Scale it very clean, and wipe it, but do not let water come near it. Lay fine salt upon it, letting it lie until melted away from it; then take pepper, mace, cloves, and a little brown sugar, which rub all over the red side, and then with a few bay leaves (cut in pieces) put it into a pan, with plenty of butter, out of which the salt has been washed, to bake in a slow oven. When it is done, let the gravy be poured away, and take out the fish, lay it on a clean cloth to drain, put it into your pots, press it as close down as you possibly can, and pour clarified butter over it.

D

CAVEACH MACKEREL.

Take twelve mackerel when in high season, open them at the belly, and take out the roes and gills; wipe them perfectly clean on both sides, and rinse them in clean salt and water; let them drip, and rub them well inside with pepper, salt, cloves, and mace finely powdered; put the roes back into the fish, and lay them close together in a pan; then just cover them with one part vinegar and three parts water, and a quarter of a pound of butter. Bake them in a slow oven, with paper or cloth tied over the pan.

PICKLED OYSTERS.

Take three scores of fine, large, well-fed oysters, taking care not to cut them in the opening; wash them in their own liquor until quite free from small pieces of shell, and take off the black part at the vent nicely. Strain the liquor through a fine sieve, and put it into a clean saucepan, with half an ounce of white pepper and six blades of mace ; let it simmer for a quarter of an hour, then put in the oysters, and let them simmer until they begin to shrivel up; take them out quickly, and place them between two clean cloths. Increase the liquor, if you think it not sufficient, by salt and water, but do not weaken it unnecessarily. Put the oysters into a jar or into wide-necked glass bottles ; pour the liquor upon them while warm ; let them be filled to the bung when closed up, and seal the corks. They will be found extremely useful in those months when oysters are not to be got at all, and particularly at a distance from a sea-port.

COLLARED EELS.

Eels to be fit for collaring should exceed two pounds in weight. Take off the skin, cut off the head, fins, and tail, open the belly as far as the tail from the head downwards, and clean it out very nicely with a cloth; then with a sharp pen-knife lay open the back from the inside of the fish until you can get at the back-bone, which must all be taken out, as well as any other bones you can find. Then put the fish in salt and water for two hours; rub it quite dry, and spread the following ingredients well upon the inside : —

Two anchovies, well beaten.
Saltpetre   -   -   -   - 1 oz.
Common salt   -   -   -   - 1 oz.
Two blades of mace.
Cayenne pepper   -   -.   - 1 oz.
Parsley, a handful chopped small.

Roll up the fish, beginning at the tail, as closely as you can, and sew it up in a cloth and boil it for ten minutes; let it simmer ten more; then take it out, and put it into a jar. Boil one part vinegar and two parts water together with black pepper-corns and a little salt, and when cool pour this pickle over the fish, and press it down into it so as to exclude the air. It will keep a long time thus; or you may bake it in a slow oven if it is intended to be eaten immediately.

POTTED SPRATS.

The small fish, or refuse of sprats, are very good if served in the following manner : —

Wash the fish well, take off the heads, and draw the small gut out ; wash them a second time in salt and water, and dry them between two clean cloths ; then lay them in an earthen pan with pepper, salt, and a little pounded mace between each layer, and a few bay leaves on every alternate one, and so on until the pan is nearly full ; then add water and vinegar, and tie paper over them, and put them to bake in a slow oven. When cold they are fit for use. They should be taken off the top, so as always to leave gravy enough to cover them, and thus the last of them will be better than the first.

PICKLED SALMON.

It is impossible for any private person to pickle salmon to equal that which comes to

London in kits, and is termed Newcastle salmon, because he cannot, without considerable expense, provide the fine rich liquor in which it is preserved, and which can only be obtained by the wholesale trader. But the following process will be found to answer. Take a salmon, wipe it well on the scaly side, take out the gills totally, and cut off a piece of the tail part, about six or eight inches long. Split it (beginning at the head) open at the back and through the belly, making two sides of it; put aside the liver and clean the inside well with a cloth, and strew fine salt over the fish: thus let it lie three hours if it be a ten-pound fish, and let the tail remain two hours longer in salt. Cleanse it in fresh water, and then dry it well, cut it into pieces, leaving a handsome head or jowl, and place them on the drainer of your fish kettle, which must be just covered with water, and no more, when put on the fire. Mix half a pint of vinegar with the water, and let it boil very slowly ten minutes, and after that it must only simmer until the fish

will easily leave the bone; take it out, and
when nearly cold, lay it in your deep dish.
Skim off the top as much liquor as you think
will cover the salmon, and tying up the liver in
a piece of linen rag, let it simmer half an hour
along with black pepper-corns in the liquor,
which, when lukewarm, may be poured over
the fish.   The salmon must be laid very closely
in the dish, and gently taken out when wanted
for use: the remainder should always be left
covered with the liquor, which will keep it
much longer than if it is allowed to lie bare.
Where it can be had, a little fennel should be
sent to table with the salmon.

POTTED EELS.

The eels for this purpose should be about
three quarters or a pound each, and must be
skinned, and the heads and fins cut off. Split
them open at the back, and take out the bones
as clearly as you can, and also the gut; wash
them very clean, and wipe them well. Then

put sweet butter into a small saucepan, with
white pepper and mace beaten fine, and cayenne
pepper; simmer all together for ten minutes,
and set them aside. Scatter table salt over the
fish, and let them lie one hour; then wash them
quite free from the salt, and wipe them again
well; cut them into junks two or three inches
long, and put them into the saucepan to the
butter, and simmer all together. Take them
out carefully without breaking them, and put
them while warm into pots as closely as you
can; then pour a little of the butter over each
pot among the eels, and when they are cold fill
them up with clarified butter, and they will be
excellent.

DEVILLED SHRIMPS.

Take shrimps that have been boiled, and
pick them very clean, saving the heads and
skins, which must be put into a saucepan, with
butter, mace, a little salt, and cayenne pepper,
and simmered ten minutes. Strain the butter

through a fine sieve, and having cleaned the
saucepan, return it over the fire one minute,
with the shrimps in it; just let it boil, and
then take out the shrimps, which place in your
pots with care, and as they cool press them
closely down ; pour over them the butter,
equally dividing it, and when cold put more
butter on them.

POTTED TROUT.

Your fish should be very fresh for this purpose. Scale them well, cut off the heads, fins,
and tails, and wipe them well with a clean
cloth dipped in salt and water; next open them
to the vent, and take out the guts, saving the
roes, if there be any ; wash them in strong salt
and water for ten minutes at least, and dry
them well. Next take mace, cloves, table salt
(very little), and white pepper; beat them all
as fine as possible, and rub them well into the
inside of each fish ; replace the roes (which of
course must be well washed), and place the

fish cut to their size into your pots; tie paper
over them, and bake them in a slow oven; take
them out when done enough, and when cool
press the fish well, and when cold pour clarified
butter over them. In this way Tench, Gray-
ling, or any other delicate fish, may be potted.

SMOKED MEATS.

Much has been said in favour of Westphalia
hams, Dutch beef, Hungarian beef, &c. (I allude
to those which we import.) For many years
I was a wholesale purchaser of these articles
in the port of London, and finding that in
many cases I could not rely on their quality, I
set about the imitation of them, and, having
obtained much useful information on the sub-
ject, after repeated trials, I produced goods
which, in the opinion of my customers, were
quite as fine, nay, superior to most I could
purchase. Nor is this astonishing, for it is
admitted that British meat is better bred
and fed, and more neatly slain and dressed,

than any others, and the ingredients for curing are easily procured. Cold weather, from the end of October to the end of March, is the best season for the process.

WESTPHALIA HAMS.

Get the hams cut in the shape of Westphalias as nearly as you can, viz. long and narrow, and approaching to a point at the end, and put them under a board made purposely, heavily pressed down to flatten them. About four days after killed, rub them all over with common rough salt, particularly about the hip-bone and knuckle joints. Having brushed off the salt (which should remain on for a day and night), and dried the hams with a coarse cloth, rub thoroughly and equally into each, one ounce of saltpetre, powdered finely, and let it lie so for twenty-four hours, then take

Saltpetre	-	-	-	- 1 oz.
Common salt	-	-	-	- $\frac{1}{2}$ lb.
Bay salt	-	-	-	- $\frac{1}{4}$ lb.
Coarse sugar	-	-	-	- 1 lb.

Make them hot in a pan — but be careful not to melt them — and rub them well in, while hot, all over the fleshy and rind sides, and finish with half a pound more of common salt. Let them lie thus until a brine appears, and then with plenty of bay-leaves, strewed both under and over, turn them every day, and rub and baste them well with the brine for the space of three weeks; then take them out of pickle and immerse them in cold spring water for twenty-four hours; let them drip; wipe them well with a cloth; rub hog's blood, that has coagulated, all over them, and put them to smoke for a week, well smothered.

DUTCH BEEF.

Choose about eight pounds of the buttock or other tender part, without bone; rub it thoroughly with eight ounces of the coarsest sugar you can get, and let it lie in an earthen pan two days, then wipe it well with a cloth, and rub in the following:—

Saltpetre, beaten finely	-		- 6 oz.
Bay salt ditto	-	-	- 1 lb.
Common salt	-	-	- 1 lb.

Let it lie sixteen days, and rub and turn it in the brine every other day ; then take it out, and wipe it dry, and having bruised two ounces of juniper berries, make them totally disappear by rubbing them in all over it. Then sew it up in a coarse cloth, without wiping it, and suspend it in your chimney, where you may smoke it eight days or more, turning it every second day, that the brine may not settle in one part more than in another.

HUNGARIAN BEEF.

Take ten pounds, or thereabouts, of fine fat short rib or sirloin of beef that has been killed four or five days; rub it thoroughly over with half a pound of coarse sugar or treacle until none can be seen ; and after lying two days take

Juniper berries -	-	-	- 2 oz.
Bay salt	-	-	- $\frac{1}{2}$ lb.
Saltpetre	-	-	- 2 oz.
Sal prunelle	-	-	- 1 oz.
Common salt	-	-	- 1 lb.

all finely beaten to powder; and some bay leaves and thyme chopped small; rub them all in for an hour, and let it lie for three weeks in an earthen pan, being every day well rubbed with the brine. Then take it out and wipe it well, and plunge it into cold water for twelve hours; rub it perfectly dry, and make it a dark brown colour with bullock's blood; hang it up in gentle smoke three days, after which carry on your smoke until the meat is nearly black.

PRUSSIAN HAMS.

Take a short, thick, fat leg of pork, and, three days after it has been killed, rub it well with

Saltpetre	-	-	-	- 1 oz.
Bay salt	-	-	-	- $\frac{1}{2}$ lb.
Treacle	-	-	-	- 1 lb.
Marjoram, handful				
Thyme, ditto			chopped small;	
Bay leaves, ditto				

and keep up the rubbing and basting of it one week, turning it over every day, after

which, strew common salt over it an inch thick,
and let it lie till the salt and brine therefrom
are well mixed; then boil up the whole pickle,
and pour it very hot, but not scalding, over the
meat, and let it lie a fortnight longer, when you
may smoke it, without wiping it, for six or
seven days in a gentle heat for the first six hours,
and cool afterwards.

HAMBURGH BEEF.

Procure a piece of meat from the bed, or
other fleshy part; scatter common salt under
and over it, and let it lie twenty-four hours to
void the blood, then put it into the following
pickle :

Water that has been boiled	-	- 1 gallon.
Common salt -	-	-	- 1 lb.
Coarse sugar -	-	-	- 1½ lb.
Saltpetre	-	-	- 2 oz.
Vinegar (common)	-	-	- ¼ pint.

Simmer them until all are melted, and pour the
liquor over the meat, which must be placed in
a deep narrow pan, so that it may be covered

completely: it will be ready to be smoked in three weeks, but let it be well dried with a cloth, and rub pease meal all over it until you have got a coat or case on it, and, if it be well smoked, it will come out of a bright yellow cast, and will keep any length of time.

COLLARED BEEF.

Take a piece of the flank of a well-fed beast from fourteen to sixteen pounds' weight, cut it square, or rather oblong, and take off the inner skin. Make a brine of bay salt and water to float an egg, and let the meat lie covered in it for one week; then take it out, dry it well, and rub it all over with finely powdered saltpetre, and let it remain so for a week longer in the former pickle, then wipe it completely dry, and mix

White pepper, in powder -	- 1 oz.
Nutmeg, grated - -	- 1½ oz.
Mace, beaten fine - -	- 1 oz.
Cloves, ditto - - -	- 1 oz.
Four shalots, shredded fine.	

Let these be beaten into a paste (in a mortar)
and evenly spread completely over the inner
side of the meat. Roll up the beef as closely
as possible, and tie it tightly round with tape,
and hang it up to smoke for a fortnight.
After which, if you choose to boil a part,
let it be in water, with one tenth part of the
commonest vinegar, until it is quite tender.

SPICED BACON.

Select a side or middle of delicate pork, take
out all the bones, and put it in a pan of water
for twelve hours to extract the blood, changing
the water three times, or as often as it becomes
red. Then put it into the following pickle: —

Water	-	-	- 1 gallon.
Common salt	-	-	- 1 lb.
Sal prunelle	-	-	- $\frac{1}{4}$ lb.
Coarse sugar	-	-	- 1 lb.

for sixteen days; take it out, wipe it well, and
shred sage and bay leaves (the stalks having

been carefully taken out) so small that they are more like a powder, to which, when well mixed, add white pepper, and strew these well over the inside part of the meat ; roll it very tightly up, and tie string round it three inches apart, and knot the string at every round, that when fillets are cut off for cooking, the remainder of the collar may be confined. Smoke it well for a fortnight, and it will be a great rarity, and excellent in quality.

NEATS' TONGUES SMOKED.

Rub six tongues well with sugar for two days, then rub them well with common salt and saltpetre for two days more, apart from the sugar. Take then

Water, and as much porter	-		- 1 quart.
Saltpetre	-	-	-	- $\frac{1}{4}$ lb.
Bay salt	-	-	-	- 2 lbs.
Common salt	-	-	-	- 2 lbs.

and with the sugar first used make a hot pickle,

which skim well, and pour over the tongues
which must be laid in a deep narrow pan, and
completely covered. Let them lie for eight days
more, and they will be fit for use in any way.
If you smoke them, wipe them well, and turn
them in the chimney four or five times for
five days.

RUSSIAN POLONY

Should be made of hard old Belfast hams,
which are easily procured, and from beef, which
is to be prepared in the following manner. Take
a small round, or part of a large one, of ox
beef (for the udder of the cow cannot be used
here); rub it all over with common salt, and
scatter more under and over it; so let it lie
four days. Then wipe it, and put it into the
following pickle, in a deep pan: —

Water that has boiled	-		- 1 gallon.
Common salt	-	-	- 2 lbs.
Saltpetre	-	-	- 2 ozs.
Bay salt	-	-	- 2 lbs.

Let it lie fourteen days more covered with pickle. Take it out and wipe it well; tie string round it, and hang it to smoke for twenty days in a powerful smoke, turning it often; and when taken from the chimney, hang it in a warm dry room three weeks longer to harden. Take then an equal weight of ham and beef, and cut off all the hard fat, which put aside. Cut up the meat in small pieces, and leave no skinny or fibrous parts in it. Beat each separately in a mortar until very fine, and work it into a consistence; being completely mixed, add finely ground black pepper, and then cut your hard fat up into small squares the size of a pea, and mix these generally and equally throughout the mass. Dissolve gum-dragon so that it is very thick, and work it amongst the meat until the paste has become just soft enough to stuff the skins, which must be the largest you can get, and taken from large oxen. Great care must be taken in filling them, so that the meat may soon become united into a solid mass, which can only be effected by force; the skins must then be well tied up, and hung to dry: they should be smoked for a fortnight, and kept three months in a dry closet.

LEG OF MUTTON HAMS.

If this process be accurately observed, the result will be a splendid treat, and such as is not to be purchased at any price in the shops.

Select a short, thick, round leg of wether mutton about fourteen pounds' weight. Rub it thoroughly for twenty minutes or half an hour with coarse sugar, and let it lie twelve hours, turning it three times. Then plunge it into the following pickle, with what sugar you have on the dish: —

Bay salt	-	-	-	- $\frac{1}{2}$ lb.
Common salt	-	-	-	- 1 lb.
Saltpetre	-	-	-	- 1 oz.
Juniper berries	-	-	-	- 2 oz.
Thyme	-	-	-	- 1 handful.
Bay leaves	-	-	-	- 1 ditto.
Soft water	-	-	-	- 2 quarts.

These must be simmered together one hour,
and used when lukewarm.   Let it remain in
this pickle three weeks; take it out, but do not
wipe it.   It may then be smoked, but insist on
its being turned frequently, sometimes shank
upwards, and *vice versa,* for a fortnight, in a
strong regular fume.   When cold, put it into a
calico bag, and hang it up in the kitchen until
you want to dress it.   Then bury it in the bag
in a dry garden soil for twenty hours or so ;
and take care, when it is boiled, to put plenty
of bay leaves, thyme, and marjoram into the
pot along with it.

SMOKED GEESE.

When geese are cheapest, which is generally after Christmas, take as many as you
please, only seeing that they are fresh, and not
in the least damp or muggy.   They must then be
cleanly drawn and picked from pen feathers, and
wiped well out with a cloth dipped in strong
salt and water; after which they must be
immersed in the following :—

For six Geese.

Coarse sugar	-	-	- 2 lbs.
Bay salt	-	-	- 1 lb.
Saltpetre	-	-	- 3 oz.
Sage, finely beaten	-	-	- 1 handful.
Three shalots, ditto.			
Bay leaves, ditto	-	-	- 2 handfuls.

These ingredients must be boiled altogether ten minutes, and afterwards simmered half an hour; when cold, pour them over the geese, which must be turned often, and, if possible, kept covered with the pickle. Let them remain forty-eight hours. Then take them out and let them drip (do not wipe them), and rub cayenne pepper plentifully inside each until it adheres. Smoke them three days and nights in a cool smoke, and hang each up in a calico bag in your kitchen, and when wanted for table dissect them, and broil them over a clear fire.

COLLARED BREAST OF VEAL.

Take a large breast of fat veal, and cut the edges square, take out the bones neatly, and let it lie in salt and water six hours; dry it, and then make a paste of

Brown sugar	-	-	-	- 1 lb.
Mace, beaten	-	-	-	- 1 oz.
Cloves, ditto	-	-	-	- 1 oz.
Sweet marjoram		-	-	- 1 handful.
Parsley	-	-	-	- 1 ditto.
Six anchovies.				

Strew it all over the veal, and roll it up into a collar; sew it up tightly in a cloth, and let it lie twenty-four hours; let it be simmered (not boiled) for half an hour, and then hang it up to dry for a day and night. Smoke it four or five days and nights, and keep it in a dry room.

PICKLED PORK.

Cut your pork into pieces convenient for placing in your pickling tub, and, where it can be done, take out the bone, being careful that your vessel be perfectly sweet and sound; for otherwise it will not answer the purpose. Rub every piece well with saltpetre, then take one part of bay salt and two parts of common salt, and after rubbing each piece thoroughly, place them down, and cover them completely with common salt. The closer the meat is stowed the better, and keep the sides of the tub well filled up with salt. Meat thus cured will keep any length of time, without losing its excellence.

POTTED NEATS' TONGUES.

This is a peculiar but excellent mode of preparing tongues, and well deserves a trial.

Pickle the tongues as you would for boiling or smoking (see page 47.). Boil them until they are tender, and, when cool enough, peel them nicely, and pare off the root considerably, then take,

For Six Tongues,

Mace, beaten finely	-	-	- $\frac{1}{2}$ oz.
Cloves, ditto	-	-	- 1 oz.
White pepper	-	-	- 1 oz.

Rub these well into the tongues, and lay them

in an earthen pot to bake, with plenty of
sweet lard or butter to cover them; put over
them a crust of brown flour, and commit them
to a slow oven. When done, pour off the
gravy, which may be eaten with them; but
the butter may be saved, and will serve for the
same purpose again.

POTTED BEEF AS VENISON.

Choose a piece of lean beef from the buttock,
or other part that has no bone in it; rub it all
over with saltpetre, and let it lie twelve hours,
then salt it thoroughly with bay salt and common salt in equal parts, well blended. Place
it in a pot that will only just contain it;
let it be completely covered with water, and
remain thus four days; then wipe it well with
a cloth, and rub it with pepper beaten to a
powder; lay it into a pot without any liquor;
put over it a crust of brown flour, and let
it bake like large loaves six or seven hours;

then take it out, and when it is cool enough pick out all the strings and skins, and beat it in a stone mortar finely. The seasoning must be mace, cloves, and nutmeg, reduced to a fine powder; and add a little melted butter in which flour has been absorbed; put it down in pots as closely as you can, and pour clarified butter over it.

TO PICKLE LOBSTERS.

Let the fish be quite freshly boiled, split them, and take out the flesh of the tails and claws as entire as it can be ; sprinkle over it a good seasoning of cayenne, pounded mace, and nutmeg, and press it on to them with the back of a spoon, pack the whole closely in jars or deep potting pans, and fill them up with the best vinegar, to each pint of which it will be an improvement to add a couple of spoonsful of Chili vinegar, or twice as much of fine cucumber vinegar, made without any mixture of onion. Cover the surface nearly half an inch deep with salad oil, and tie a thick paper over the jars. Another method of pickling lobsters is to boil the vinegar with a little salt, and plenty of white pepper-corns, ginger, mace, and some nutmeg sliced, for five minutes, and to let it become cold; then to lay in the fish, and heat it through very gently, without allowing it to boil, which would render it hard; it is then laid into the jars, and the pickle, when nearly cold, is poured upon it. This is a convenient mode of keeping lobsters, or the remains of them when the weather is warm, or when they are not wanted for immediate eating.

HERRINGS PICKLED OR COLLARED.

Scrape off all the scales, cut off the fins, and cleanse the insides of the fish thoroughly; take out the bones of the back, and scrape the little bones from the sides; then put the herrings into plenty of cold water, and wash them well. Drain, and wipe them dry. Mix some

pounded mace, grated nutmeg, fine salt, and
cayenne pepper, with some good butter; spread
a portion over the inside of each of the herrings; roll them up tightly; bind them with
tape or twine; put them into a jar; cover
them with equal parts of vinegar and water;
tie thick paper over, and bake them two hours
in a cool oven.

PICKLED MUSCLES.

Boil the muscles as for eating, open them,
free them from the weeds, put them into a
stone jar, and pour boiling on them their own
liquor, mixed with an equal portion of highly
spiced vinegar. They will remain good a long
time if closely covered from the air.

KIPPER'D SALMON.

Procure a perfectly fresh salmon of ten
pounds weight or thereabouts, wipe it very
clean, split it open at the back, beginning at

the head, down to the tail; take out the gills
neatly, remove the entrails, and take care you
do not break the gall; then with a dry cloth
clear it from blood, and immerse it in a pickle
composed of bay and common salt in equal
proportions, and cold spring water, strong
enough to float an egg When it has laid thus
twelve hours, hang it up to drip for six hours,
then wipe it dry on the scaly side, particularly
at the roots of the fins and tail, and laying it
in a tray or earthen pan, rub the red side
equally all over with the following well-blended
mixture :

Coarse sugar -	-	-	- $1\frac{1}{2}$ lb.
Bay salt -	-	-	- $\frac{1}{4}$ lb.
White pepper	-	-	- 1 oz.
Mace, finely beaten -	-	-	- $\frac{1}{2}$ oz.
Nutmeg -	-	-	- 1 oz.

As soon as the sugar is dissolved, turn the fish
over, and rub the outside for half an hour with
the liquor; repeat this daily until the close of
the fourth day, when you may take it up, wipe
it, and hang it to dry in a current of air twenty-

four hours. This done, smoke it three days and
nights in a constant fume from oak and beech,
or birch sawdust, with plenty of dried fern
well smothered with the dust to prevent its
blazing. Take it out of your chimney, and
hang it in a dry, airy place to get cold. After
twenty-four hours have elapsed, you may broil
slices, and will find it excellent.

RED SALMON

(AS IN GLOUCESTERSHIRE, SOUTH WALES, ETC.).

Take a fine large fresh salmon of twenty
pounds weight, wipe it well, cut it open at the
belly from the gills down to three inches below
the vent, and taking away all the inside, wipe out
the fish perfectly dry. Lay it belly upwards,
and rub the inside all along the back-bone
with

Saltpetre, in powder	-	-	- ½ oz.
Sal prunelle	-	-	- ½ oz.
Bay salt	-	-	- 1 oz.

In four hours afterwards lay the fish in a large
pan, and cover it with common salt; let it lie

twenty-four hours, then turn it over and let it remain as much longer ; take it out of the salt, wipe the outside well, and lay inside

Coarse sugar	-	-	-	- 1 lb.
Treacle -	-	-	-	- 1 lb.
Bay leaves, shredded fine		-		- 1 oz.

Tie it round with pack-thread, and turn it two or three times every day, letting it lie upon a dish for six days. Wash it well in salt and water inside and outside, and hang it up by the tail to drain twelve hours ; wipe it then perfectly dry, and smoke it with oak-dust and dry cow-dung at least a week; fill the inside with clean oat-straw, and keep it in an airy, dry room ; you may cut it as wanted, like hung beef, &c., and need not fear its keeping good for twelve months.

WESTPHALIA BACON.

Take a middle of prime pork (a side with the hand and ham cut out), with the ribs in, lay it in a salting trough with common salt for twelve or fourteen hours, take it out, wipe it dry; wash out the trough, and lay the meat again in it. Boil the following ten minutes: —

River water	- -	- 1 gallon.
Bay salt, pounded	- -	- 2 lbs.
Common salt	- -	- 2 lbs.
Saltpetre	- - -	- 2 ozs.
Coarse sugar	- -	- 2 lbs.
Bay leaves, chopped small	-	- 1 handful.

Skim it well, and when cold, pour it over the pork; rub it in well twice a day, turning it often for fourteen days. Take it out of pickle, wipe it dry with cloths, and hang it up twenty-four hours in the air, after which you may smoke it three weeks at least.

BEEF HAMS.

Take the leg of a prime young Welsh heifer, or of an ox, rub it well with common salt, and let it lie a day and a night to extract the blood; then wipe it dry, and put it under a press to flatten it, and cut it in the shape of a common

F

ham. For every twelve pounds of beef, allow

Coarse sugar	-	-	-	- 1 lb.
Common salt	-	-	-	- 1 lb.
Bay salt	-	-	-	- 1 lb.
Saltpetre	-	-	-	- 1 oz.

Rub this mixture in well, in all parts, for a month, turning the meat every day, at least. Take it then out of pickle, rub it dry, and give it a good coat of coarse oatmeal and bran mixed, which will adhere by friction with the hand. Smoke it as you would hams, hung beef, &c., not less than a month.

WESTMORELAND HAMS.

Procure a leg of well-fed pork, about twenty pounds weight; rub it all over with three ounces of saltpetre, and let it lie fourteen hours. Then take

Stale porter or beer		-	- 2 quarts.
Common salt	-	-	- 2 lbs.
Coarse sugar	-	-	- 2 lbs.
Bay salt, pounded	-	-	- 1 lb.

Boil and skim it well, and pour it hot over the meat. In this pickle it must remain one month, being well rubbed and turned at least every other day. Then take it out, rub it dry, and roll it half an hour in malt dust, or, in case you cannot get it, in oatmeal; when it has well adhered, smoke the ham three weeks, and directly it is taken from the chimney put on another coat of quick-lime, made into a paste with hot water; let it remain a week, and subsequently hang it in a dry, but not warm, room.

BRITISH AMERICAN HAMS.
(A RECIPE FROM QUEBEC.)

Take a leg of pork of sixteen to eighteen pounds weight, rub one ounce of sal prunelle well into it in all parts, and let it lie twenty-four hours. Then prepare the following pickle:—

Bay salt - - -	- 12 oz.
Common salt - -	- 10 oz.
Treacle - - -	- 2 lbs.
Saltpetre - - -	- 1½ oz.
Sage, chopped small -	- 1 handful.
Garlic, ditto - -	- 3 heads.
Vinegar - - -	- 2 quarts.

When it has boiled and been well skimmed, pour it while hot over the meat, and rub in well every day for ten days; then let it lie, turning it frequently, ten days longer. Take it out of the pickle, dry it well, and hang it to smoke three weeks.

HUNG BEEF.

Bury a piece of fine fat beef in the snow for a fortnight, or hang it up to get tender as long as you think fit; wash it well in strong salt and water, and dry it well with cloths. For about fifteen pounds of beef make a pickle of

Bay salt	-	-	-	- 2 lbs.
Coarse sugar		-	-	- 1 lb.
Common salt		-	-	- 2 lbs.
Saltpetre	-	-	-	- 4 oz.
River water		-	-	- 3 quarts.

Let it boil and be well skimmed. Take one pint of common vinegar, and rub it all into the meat, and pour the pickle while warm over all, and let it remain perfectly immersed fourteen days. Take it up and dry it well. If you prefer it without being smoked, let it hang near the kitchen chimney for a week, and then put it in a paper bag, and keep it in a dry and airy room. Otherwise, smoke it three weeks with oak sawdust, and it will improve by keeping.

CALF'S HEAD BRAWN.

(FROM MISS ACTON'S " MODERN COOKERY.")

A fine large calf's head with the skin on is best adapted to this purpose. Take out the brains, and bone it entirely, or let the butcher do this. Rub a little fine salt over it, and let it drain for ten or twelve hours. Next wipe it dry, and rub each half well in every part with three quarters of an ounce of saltpetre (or with an ounce, should the head be very large), mixed with an ounce and a half of brown sugar, four ounces of common salt, and three of bay salt, all reduced to a fine powder. Turn the head in this pickle for four or five days, rubbing it a little each time; then pour over it four ounces of treacle (eight ounces for the whole head), and continue to turn it every day, and baste it with the brine very frequently, for a month; then hang it for a night to drain, fold each part separately in brown paper, and send it to be smoked from three to four weeks. When wanted for table, wash and scrape one half of it very clean, but do not soak it; lay it with the rind downwards into a saucepan or stew-pan, which will hold it easily, and cover it well with cold water, as it will swell considerably in the cooking. Let it heat rather slowly; skim it thoroughly when it first begins to simmer, and boil it as gently as possible from an hour and three-quarters to a couple of hours, or more should it not then be perfectly tender quite through; for, unless sufficiently boiled, the skin, which greatly resembles brawn, will be unpleasantly tough when cold. When the fleshy side of the head is done, which will be twenty minutes or half an hour sooner than the outside, pour the water from it, leaving so much only in the saucepan as will just cover the gelatinous part, and simmer it till this is thoroughly tender. The head thus cured is very highly flavoured, and most excellent eating. The receipt for it is altogether new. It will be seen that the foregoing proportion of ingredients (with the exception of the treacle), is for one half of the head only, and must be doubled for a whole one.

BOHEMIAN BRAWN SMOKED.

Take the head, ears, and feet of a porker of eight or ten stone weight; boil them in strong salt and water till quite tender, take out every bone, cut them in small pieces, and blend with the mass

White pepper -	-	-	- 1½ oz.
Mace, beaten fine	-	-	- 1 oz.
Bay salt	-	-	- 4 oz.
Three large shalots, shredded.			

Then take a piece of the belly of pork, about eight pounds weight, cut in a square or an oblong form; lay it in plenty of common salt for twelve hours, after which, wipe it dry, and

spread upon it the minced meat.   Roll it up as
tight as you can, binding it with tape, and sew
a coarse cloth round it, and over the ends.
Lay it in a pan of cold water, and let it simmer
by the fire three hours, at least; then take it
out and let it become cold, and the next day
take off the cloth, tie coarse paper round it,
and let it hang to smoke fourteen days.

A WARWICKSHIRE HAM.

The finest flavoured and mellowest ham I
ever partook of was cured in Warwickshire,
from the following receipt.   It weighed twenty-
seven pounds, and was cut from a hog that had
been *singed* instead of scalded.

Rub the leg of pork with two ounces of saltpetre finely beaten in all parts, particularly
about the hip-joint, and let it lie twenty-four
hours.   Then take

Rain or river water -	-	- 1 gallon.
Pale dried malt	-	- 1 peck.
Sugar or treacle	-	- 1 lb.
Bay salt, broken	-	- $1\frac{1}{2}$ lb.

| Common salt | - | - | - 2½ lbs. |
| Shalots or onions in slices | - | | - 3 oz. |

Boil all these together ten minutes, and skim the pickle well until no more scum appears; pour it hot over the meat, and let the grains remain, covering it until they begin to be sticky, when they may be drained in a hair sieve and dismissed. Keep the ham well covered with the pickle, and turned and rubbed every day for three weeks, when it may be taken out, dried with cloths, and smoked three weeks or a month. Put it in a box with malt dust all around it, and cover it from the air with sand that has been dried in an oven for a week.

LARDED FLANK OF BEEF SMOKED.

Take about a dozen pounds weight of the thick flank of beef, bone it neatly, take off the skin, and rub it all over on both sides with

Bay salt, finely beaten	-	-	- 2 oz.
Sal prunelle	-	-	-	- 2 oz.
Saltpetre	-	-	-	- 2 oz.

Coarse sugar	-	-	- 12 oz.
Common salt	-	-	- 1 lb.

Let the meat lie eight days in this mixture, and turn it every day; then wipe it very clean, and cut thin slices of sweet fat bacon, from which the rind has been separated. Strew the following mixture all over one side of the beef: —

Cloves, beaten to a powder	-	- $\frac{1}{4}$ oz.
Mace, ditto	-	- $\frac{1}{4}$ oz.
Nutmeg, ditto	-	- $\frac{1}{2}$ oz.
Parsley, boiled and chopped fine		- 1 handful.
Sweet herbs, ditto	-	- 1 handful.

Then lay the slices of bacon on the spices, and roll up the meat as tightly as possible, bind it with broad tape, and smoke it a fortnight. Boil it till tender, adding half a pint of vinegar to the water; when cold, cut it across. It will be curiously marbled, and of delicious flavour.

CALF'S HEAD SMOKED.

Procure a fine large head with the scalp on, lay it open completely at the front, and take out all the bones, the brain, and palate.

Wash it well in salt and water, then split the tongue, and put the whole in a strong pickle of salt and water six hours. Take it out and dry it well, then steep it in hot water twenty minutes; dry it again, and rub the following well all over the inside, at the same time filling the cavities : —

Sweet ham or bacon, well pounded	-	2 lbs.
White pepper	- -	- 1 oz.
Mace, finely beaten -	- -	- $\frac{1}{2}$ oz.
Bay salt, ditto	- -	- 1 oz.
Beef suet, chopped fine	-	- 4 oz.
Parsley, boiled and chopped fine		- 1 handful.

Wrap the head tightly up in a cloth, and bind it with tape; set it in a pan of salt and water on the fire, and let it boil gently two hours; then take it out and lay it on a sieve to drain, and afterwards hang it up in your chimney, and smoke it a week, having taken off the cloth and substituted strong paper. It must be boiled when wanted until it is quite tender, and permitted to get cold, and should then be cut across in slices. It will not fail to realise the anticipations of the most fastidious.

COLLARED BREAST OF MUTTON.

Take a fine large well-fed breast of mutton,
remove the skin and all the bones, wash it
well in salt and water, wipe it dry and strew
the following mixture plentifully over it : —

Mace, beaten fine	-	-	- $\frac{1}{2}$ oz.
White pepper	-	-	- $\frac{1}{2}$ oz.
Nutmeg, beaten fine	-	-	- 1 oz.
Bay salt, ditto	-	-	- 3 oz.

Roll it up, with a tape tied tightly round it,
and set it on the fire in cold water with some
salt in it, and plenty of bay leaves, and let it
simmer twenty minutes.   Then take it out,
hang it to drip, and, when quite cold and solid,
smoke it ten days.   Slices of this collar, when
broiled, will be most excellent with the ad-
dition of a little cayenne and catsup.

SIDE OF A BUCK COLLARED AND SMOKED.

Hang a side of male venison in a current of
air as long as the weather will permit, wipe it

well with a cloth, take out all the bones and
sinews, and remove the outer skin. Rub a
pint of vinegar well into it in all parts, and
cut it into three or four pieces for collars.
Then from slices of sweet fat bacon with the
rind off, cut slips half an inch in breadth, and
insert them neatly in the venison about three
inches apart. Then rub the following mixture
equally over the surface of all the collars : —

White pepper - - -	- 4 oz.
Cloves, beaten fine - -	- 1½ oz.
Mace, ditto - - -	- 2 oz.
Bay salt, ditto - - -	- 1 lb.
Common salt, ditto - -	- 1 lb.
Coarse sugar, ditto - -	- 1 lb.

Roll up the collars tightly, and put them into
a deep jar with plenty of bay leaves and any
seasoning you may have remaining, and cover
them with clarified butter. Let them be baked
in a slow oven till tender, and, when cold,
pour melted mutton suet over them to exclude
the air, and tie close down with bladder and
leather. When wanted for use, set the jar in
a saucepan of boiling water ten minutes, you

can then take out a collar whole and make up the others safe again. Either hot or cold, this will be highly esteemed, and but few persons are aware how delicious this generally styled common part of venison may be made.

If you intend to smoke a collar or two, do not bake them, but put them into a chimney and let them remain ten days amidst a constant fume of beech wood and dried fern, and put them into paper bags and hang up in a dry room.

A MARBLED GOOSE.

Take a fine mellow ox-tongue out of pickle, cut off the root and horny part at the tip, wipe it dry and boil it till it is quite tender, then peel it nicely, cut a deep slit in it the whole length, and lay a fair proportion of the following mixture within it : —

Mace, finely beaten	-	-	- $\frac{1}{2}$ oz.
Nutmeg, ditto -	-	-	- $\frac{1}{2}$ oz.
Cloves, ditto -	-	-	- $\frac{1}{2}$ oz.

Two table spoonfuls salt.

Twelve Spanish olives, well pounded without stones.

Then take a barn-door fowl and a fine large goose; take from them all the bones. Lay the tongue inside the fowl — rub the latter outside with seasoning, and, having ready some slices of ham divested of the rind, wrap them tightly round the fowl — put these, again, inside the goose with the remainder of the seasoning, and sew it up, then make all very secure and in natural shape with a piece of new linen and tape, and put it into an earthern pan that will just contain it with plenty of clarified butter, and bake it two hours and a half in a slow oven; then take it out, and when cold, take out the goose, and set it in a sieve to drain; take off the butter and hard fat, which put again by the fire to melt, adding, if requisite, more clarified butter. Wash and wipe out the jar or pan, put the bird again into it, and take care that it is well covered with the warm butter; then tie the jar down with bladder and leather. When wanted for table, it must be treated as the venison, to extricate it from the butter, and sent to table cold when it has been taken out of the cloth. This receipt needs only to be published to be practised.

A YOUNG PIG COLLARED.

Take a nice, short, plump pig about ten weeks old, that has been well cleaned and drest; cut off the neck close to the shoulder, split it down the back, and take out all the bones. Lay it in cold water twelve hours, changing the water as often as it becomes red; take it out, wipe it dry, and strew the following mixture well over the insides of both collars : —

Table salt - - -	- 12 oz.
White pepper - - -	- 1 oz.
Mace, beaten fine - -	- 1 oz.
Cloves, ditto - - -	- 1 oz.
Nutmeg, ditto - - -	- 1 oz.

Roll them up as tightly as possible in linen, and tying tape closely round, boil them until tender in the following liquor : —

White wine vinegar - -	- 3 pints.
Ginger, sliced - -	- 2 oz.
Sage, chopped - -	- 1 handful.
Bay leaves, ditto - -	- 1 ditto.

adding water only sufficient to cover them. Then take them up, and when nearly cold tighten the fillets as much as possible, and lay them singly in deep jars. Pour the liquor they were boiled in over them, adding vinegar if needful, and tie them closely down with bladder.

BOLOGNA SAUSAGES.

Take a pound of lean beef, the same weight of ham, of pork, and of bacon fat. Cut them into small pieces, and beat them together in a mortar until of a fine paste. Add to this

Mace, beaten fine	-	- $\frac{1}{2}$ oz.
White pepper	-	- 1 oz.
Bay salt, beaten fine	-	- 2 oz.
Two fine heads of garlic, shredded very fine.		
Six bay leaves,	ditto.	

Blend these well with the meat, and fill large skins, pressing it down very closely, and tying them tight; with a pin prick the skins a little to prevent their bursting, and let them boil gently three hours. Set them on a cloth to cool, turning them half round two or three times, lest the internal moisture settle too much and partially. When cold hang them up in a chimney, and smoke them a week with oak dust. Keep them in a dry room.

COLLARED HARE.

Hang up a fine hare until it begins to turn, then case it, take off the head and neck, empty the inside with care, wipe it clean and dry, and take out all the bones. Shape it neatly for a collar; then lard it with strips of sweet fat bacon, and rub it well on both sides with the following paste: —

Stale white bread, grated fine	-	- 1 ll
Mace, beaten fine	- -	- $\frac{1}{2}$ oz.
Cloves, ditto	- - -	- $\frac{1}{2}$ oz.
White pepper	- - -	- 1 oz.
Table salt	- - -	- 2 oz.
Yolks of four eggs, well beaten up.		
Sweet herbs, chopped fine	-	- 1 handful.

Lay the remainder on the inner surface and roll up the collar tightly, bind it well, and put it with butter into a deep jar that will just hold it. Take care that it is covered with butter, and bake it till tender in a slow oven. Then take it out of the oven, let it become cold, and if requisite add butter to cover it, and tie it over with bladder.

SALMON COLLARED.

Take a fresh salmon of about eight pounds weight, wipe and scale it well; cut off the head and tail, and all the fins; then split it open at the back, take out the inside and all the bones, scatter fine salt over it, and let it lie twelve hours. Then wash it well, dry it between two cloths, and lay equally over the inner surface the following : —

Twenty oysters, well scalded and beaten to a paste.
Yolks of six eggs, boiled hard.
Four anchovies, well pounded.

Mace	ditto	-	- $\frac{1}{2}$ oz.
White pepper	ditto	-	- 1 oz.
Stale white bread, grated		-	- 1 lb.

well blended and made into a stiff paste. Roll the salmon up in one collar, beginning at the tail, and bind it very tightly; sew it up in a cloth, and let it boil with plenty of sweet herbs, as marjoram, thyme, &c., and bay leaves, until it is sufficiently done. Put it in a deep jar, and boil up the pickle again, adding

Sliced ginger	-	-	-	- 1 oz.
Peppper-corns	-	-	-	- 1 oz.
Allspice	-	-	-	- 1 oz.

and, when cold, pour it over the fish, totally covering it; and tie close with bladder.

EXCELLENT PORTABLE SOUP.

Take the lean part of a firm ham of ten pounds weight, a leg of beef, and a leg of veal (after the round and fillet have been cut off); slice off all the meat, and chop up the bones small. Put half a pound of the best butter you can procure into a pan, with six or seven heads of celery sliced, and from which the tops have been cut off, seven or eight anchovies, and two ounces of mace, four shalots sliced, and four large-sized carrots cut into small pieces. Set these on the fire, and shake them often to prevent their burning, until the butter and juices have attained a brown colour, then pour in as much water as will cover them, and let it simmer four or five hours. Then strain it through a hair sieve into another saucepan, darken the colour if you think proper, and let it simmer by the fire until it becomes glutinous. Great care must be taken that it does not adhere to the pan and become burnt. You may now add Cayenne pepper and salt to your taste, and pour it out on dishes a quarter of an inch thick ; and when nearly cold cut it into cakes, which may be packed in tin cases between writing-paper, and kept in a cool dry place until wanted.

A pint of boiling water poured into a basin on one or more of these cakes will immediately produce soup of a very superior flavour, which will be found a great convenience, especially in travelling. It is calculated to keep unimpaired in taste and quality for many months.

HERRINGS CAVEACHED BROWN.

Take a score of fresh herrings, wipe them clean and cut off the heads and tails, lay open the bellies with a sharp knife, and clean them well, reserving the roes; then take

Nutmeg, beaten fine	-	-	- 1 oz.
Mace ditto	-	-	- $\frac{1}{2}$ oz.
Cloves ditto	-	-	- 1 oz.
White pepper	-	-	- 1 oz.
Table salt	-	-	- 4 oz.

Mix these well together, wash the roes clean, season them with the above mixture, and replace them in the fish. Fry the herrings with olive oil until they are of a bright brown colour, and lay them on a cloth to dry, and, when cold, lay them carefully in oblong pots, and cover them with white wine vinegar, adding as much salad oil as will preserve the surface from the action of the atmosphere. Then tie bladder closely over the pots, and set them in a dry cool room.

DUTCH HERRING PASTE.

Select a dozen of the male or soft-roed her-rings just taken out of the pickle, cut off the heads, tails, and fins, and splitting them open at the back, take out the bones, and beat the flesh in a mortar, with

Clarified butter -   -   -   - 2 oz.
Mace beaten fine   -   -   - $\frac{1}{2}$ oz.
Cayenne pepper   -   -   - 1 oz.

When the spices are well incorporated with the fish, and the whole has become a nice paste, fill small pots, and cover them to the top with mutton suet melted; tie paper over the tops of the pots, and store them. This is preferred by many persons to anchovy paste, on account of its never becoming rancid. It is much richer, and will keep a very long time in any weather.

PICKLED OX-PALATES.

Procure a dozen palates as fresh as you can, cleanse them with a brush in salt and

water thoroughly, and dry them with a cloth.
Put them into a saucepan, with as much salt
and water as will cover them, and when it is
on the point of boiling, skim it well, and add

White pepper-corns	-	-	- 1 oz.
Cloves	-	-	- $\frac{1}{2}$ oz.
Mace	-	-	- $\frac{1}{2}$ oz.
Six bay leaves.			

Boil them gently about five hours, or until
they are perfectly tender, then take them out,
peel them, let them become quite cold, cut
them into pieces an inch square, and put them
into clean jars, with a few more bay leaves.
Strain the liquor they were boiled in into another saucepan, and add thereto half a pint of
white wine vinegar, and half a pint of any
foreign white wine. Let it simmer for five
minutes; take off the scum, and, when cold,
add it to the palates, covering them completely,
and pour salad oil over all. Then tie bladder
and leather over the jars, and put them into
your store-room.

PICKLED PIGEONS.

Split your birds open at the backs, take out the bones neatly, and season them highly with mace, cloves, salt, and pepper. Sew them up, and tie them effectually at the neck and vent. Set them in a saucepan just covered with water to boil, adding

Vinegar	-	-	-	- 1 quart.
Salt	-	-	-	- $\frac{1}{4}$ lb.
Peel of a lemon.				
Sweet herbs	-	-	-	- 1 handful.

Boil them till tender, then take them up, put them in pots, and pour over them the pickle they were boiled in. If they are intended for keeping a long time, cover them with melted mutton suet, and tie closely with bladder.

POTTED LAMPREYS.

These beautifully delicate fish are taken in large quantities in the river Severn, at Worcester, and are there potted in great perfection.

Take a score of fresh lampreys, skin them

neatly, remove the cartilage which runs along the back, lay them open at the belly down to the vent, take out the guts, and wipe them clean, then mix

White pepper	-	-	- $\frac{1}{2}$ oz.
Cayenne	-	-	- $\frac{1}{2}$ oz.
Mace, beaten fine	-	-	- $\frac{1}{2}$ oz.
Table salt	-	-	10 oz.

Lay some of this seasoning inside each fish, and place them tastefully in pots, strewing more seasoning over them, covered with clarified butter, and set them to bake in a slow oven three-quarters of an hour. Then take them out, and, if it is required, add more butter, that the fish may be completely covered. When cold, tie writing-paper over the pots, and set them in a dry cool place.

POTTED SMELTS.

Take fresh smelts, clean and gut them very carefully, cut them open at the belly, and season them lightly with mace, nutmeg, salt, and pepper. Lay them in your pots, and bake them with clarified butter from twenty minutes to three-quarters of an hour, according to their size, and when cold pour more butter over them. Tie close, &c.

POTTED PIKE.

Scale a pike well, cut off the head, tail, and fins, lay open the belly and clean it well; then mix with half a pound of the best butter, mace, Cayenne, nutmeg, salt, and white pepper, and rub the inside of the fish thoroughly with it. Tie it up with packthread, and let it bake till done enough, in abundance of good butter; when cold, take out all the bones with great care, and beat the meat in a mortar with the cold butter only (not any of the gravy), and fill your pots, covering the same with clarified butter.

POTTED LOBSTER.

Take a fine large lobster, wash it well in salt and water, and boil it in salt and water until it is sufficiently done. Then take it up and lay it on a cloth to cool; cut open the shell, take out the flesh of the tail and claws, and divide it into small pieces. Pound it thoroughly in a mortar, mixing with it, as you proceed, fresh butter, that has been clarified, mace, Cayenne, and table salt, as your taste dictates. When you have reduced all to a nice, smooth, stiff paste, fill your pots therewith and cover with clarified butter, and tie white paper over that.

POTTED MACKAREL.

Take a dozen fine fresh mackarel, wipe them well and split them open at the back down to the tail, take out the roes and wash them in salt and water, clean out the fish nicely, then cut off the heads, tails, and fins; take out the bones, and rub them well inside with a seasoning

of salt, pepper, mace, and nutmeg, all beaten
fine.   Lay in the roes again in the hollow of
the belly, and flattening them with a knife,
season them also.   Begin at the tail, and roll up
each fish separately, and bind them as collars, or
sew linen round each.   Set them in an earthen
pan to bake, covered with butter and bay
leaves; and when sufficiently done, set them to
cool.   Take them out and put them in pots,
and collecting the butter they were baked in,
set it to warm again.   Then add fresh bay
leaves to the fish in the pots, and pour the
butter over them: add more if required, and
when cold make all safe with bladder.

POTTED PIGEONS.

Take a dozen pigeons that have been killed at
least two days, draw and pick them very nicely;
cut off the heads, necks, and pinions, and after
they have been thoroughly washed in strong
salt and water, dry them with a cloth, season
them well with pepper and salt inside, sew

them up at the neck and vent, and bake them
well in butter, in a slow oven. Then take them
out and put them separately into your pots,
and cover them with clarified butter, after having used that in which they were baked, which
must be well strained.

POTTED HARE.

Hang up your hare for four or five days, then
case, open, and empty it, cleanse the inside
well, and wipe it dry with cloths. Cut it
then in pieces, and put it to bake with half a
pound of the best butter, and mace, nutmeg,
pepper, and salt, tied up in a muslin bag, and
not more water than will just cover it. When
tender take it out, and set it to cool; divest it
of all bones, sinews, and skin, and pound the
meat finely in a mortar, adding the spices and
butter (but not the gravy) with which it was
baked. When cold and solid, put it into pots,
pour clarified butter over it, and paper over
that, and set the pots in a dry cool room.

POTTED WOODCOCKS.

Pick and clean your birds nicely, but do not draw out the trail; fix the bills with small skewers to the thighs and the legs on the breasts; season them highly with mace, pepper, and salt, and put them into a deep pot with fresh butter to bake in a moderate oven. When done sufficiently, take them out to drain on a sieve, and when cold place them in pots and cover them completely with clarified butter. Tie them securely from the air with bladder and set them in a dry place.

POTTED MOOR GAME.

When the birds have hung long enough, pick and draw them well, and wipe them out clean. Season them inside and out with salt, pepper, mace, and cloves, beaten to a fine powder. Truss and roast them brown, and, when cold, put them in pots nicely fitted to their size, and pour clarified butter over them completely, only allowing the heads to protrude about one inch: these should be nicely glazed to preserve them.

POTTED VENISON

Having hung your venison as long as prudent, rub it perfectly dry and clear from mould, and let it remain in a current of air two hours. Then rub it well all over with vinegar, and in three hours afterwards with the lees or bottoms of port wine, and mace, cloves, pepper, and Cayenne, beaten fine. Let it lie four or five hours, and then put it in an earthern pan, and pour over it half a pint of port wine. Divide one pound of the best fresh butter into eight or ten lumps and lay them on the meat, tie brown paper over the pot, and put it to bake in a moderate oven till sufficiently done. Then take it out, and when cool take away the bones and strings, and beat it finely in a mortar, adding the seasoning and hard fat with which it was baked; press it down closely in pots, and pour

clarified butter well over the meat, and tie
bladder over them.

PICKLED MANGOES.

Cucumbers for this purpose must be large,
and cut from the plant before they are too ripe,
or become in the least yellow. Make an incision
at the side, and, taking out a piece of the fruit,
save it entire, and extract the seeds thoroughly;
put the cucumbers, with the pieces which
have been cut from them, into a strong pickle
of salt and water, and leave them in it for ten
days, or until they become yellow; then place
them in a pan, with thick layers of fresh vine-
leaves between them. Dissolve a little powdered alum in the brine from which they have
been taken, pour it on them, and set the pan
over a moderate fire, and keep the cucumbers at
a scalding heat for four hours at least, without
on any account allowing them to boil: by that
time they will be of a fine green colour. Drain
them on a sieve, and when cold put a stick

H

of horse-radish, some mustard seed, four cloves of garlick, and a quarter of an ounce of pepper-corns into each cucumber. Fit in the piece that was taken out, and stitch it with a needle and green silk. Then prepare the following pickle: —

Black pepper-corns	-	-	-	2 oz.
Long pepper	-	-	-	2 oz.
Sliced ginger	-	-	-	2 oz.
Mustard seed	-	-	-	4 oz.
Garlic	-	-	-	1 oz.
Mace	-	-	-	1 oz.
Cloves	-	-	-	1 oz.
Best white wine vinegar		-	-	1 gallon.

Let these boil together eight minutes. Lay the mangoes into a deep jar, and when the pickle is cold pour it on them, and tie first bladder, and then leather, closely over.

CODLINS.

Gather them when they are the size of a hen's egg, and, wrapping them singly in vine-leaves, place them in a saucepan over a slow fire, with plenty of vine-leaves between the layers, and upon the top, and water enough to cover them. Let them boil gently until the peel begins to separate from them; then take them up carefully, and drain them on a sieve, and when cool, pare them nicely, and put them again into the pan, covering them closely so that no steam can escape, and boil them until they become a nice green colour. Take them up, and let them drain till quite cold; place them in jars, and cover them with white wine vinegar; pour melted mutton suet over a strong paper floating on the vinegar, then tie first bladder, and then leather upon that, and set them in a cool dry room.

GOLDEN PIPPINS.

Select some of the largest, and most free from bruises and specks, and, laying them in a pan covered with water over a clear fire, let them simmer (not boil) until the peel starts from them; when they are tender let them cool, take off the peel, and lay them again in the water, adding half a pint of vinegar, and let them remain simmering until they look green. Take them out singly with a spoon, and set them to cool. Prepare the following pickle : —

Garlic, sliced	-	-	-	- $\frac{1}{2}$ oz.
Mustard seed	-	-	-	- 2 oz.
Mace, bruised	-	-	-	- $\frac{1}{2}$ oz.
Cloves, ditto	-	-	-	- 1 oz.
Ginger, ditto	-	-	-	- 1 oz.

Boil and skim it well, and pour it, when cold, over the pippins in jars, and cover them securely from the air.

GRAPES.

Those of the lighter shades, commonly called white grapes, are the most fit for pickling, and should be gathered when at their full growth, but before they are ripe. Separate them into small bunches, and place them lightly in a deep stone jar, with layers of vine-leaves, and pour upon them a mixture, half of bay-salt and half of common salt and water, strong enough to bear an egg ; place the jar, with bladder tied closely over it, in a saucepan of boiling water, and after it has boiled half an hour take off the bladder, and skim it well, and let it become cold. In this state the grapes must remain twenty hours; then take them out and dry them well between two cloths, excluding, as much as possible, the air.   Then take

Coarse sugar	-	-	- 1½ lb.
Soft water -	-	-	- 1½ quart.
Best white wine vinegar	-		- 3 ditto.

Boil this pickle, and skim it until perfectly clear, then let it become quite cold. Next take a clean jar, with plenty of vine-leaves, lay in it the bunches of grapes, and pour the liquor over them, but not the sediment; and be careful that your jars are full, and the fruit well covered. Then tie them down safely, and put them away in a cool place.

APRICOTS, PEACHES, AND NECTARINES.

Gather the fruit just before it begins to ripen, and reject any that is bruised, or in any respect unsound. Lay the plums in a pickle of salt and water that will float an egg, three days; then take them out, wipe them carefully, and put them in jars, and pour over them the following pickle, when cold, letting it previously be well boiled and skimmed: —

Best white wine vinegar	-	-	1 gallon.
Mace, beaten	-	-	$\frac{1}{2}$ oz.
Cloves, ditto	-	-	$\frac{1}{2}$ oz.
Nutmeg, ditto	-	-	$\frac{1}{2}$ oz.
Ginger, sliced	-	-	1 oz.
2 heads of garlic, chopped fine.			
Best Durham mustard, mixed	-	-	$1\frac{1}{2}$ pint.

Fill the jars to the top, and tie them safely down with bladder and leather. When kept twelve months, they will be rich, and very elegant pickles.

LEMON PICKLE.

With a grater not too rough rub off the rind of a dozen fine large lemons, being careful not to take at the same time any of the white part which lies underneath. Then peel off the white, cut the fruit across in the middle, and again

from the pointed ends towards the middle, about
two inches down, rub them all over with bay-salt
finely powdered, and let them dry on a dish in
a very slack oven until the juice is absorbed by
the peels. Then put them into a jar with

Mustard seed	-	-	-	$\frac{1}{2}$ pint.
4 heads of garlic, peeled.				
Mace, beaten fine		-	-	- 1 oz.
Cloves, ditto	-	-	-	- $\frac{1}{2}$ oz.
Nutmeg, ditto	-	-	-	- 1 oz.

tied up in a muslin bag, and pour over them
two quarts of boiling white wine vinegar.
Tie the jar close, and let it stand by the fire
one week, shaking it well four or five times
each day. Make the jar secure with bladder
and leather, and in four or five months it will
have lost its bitter flavour. Then proceed to
bottle it. Put both the lemons and pickle into
a hair sieve and press out all the liquor, which
you must put into a jar, and after twenty-four
hours have elapsed pour it off through muslin
into bottles, which should be immediately well
corked and made secure with sealing-wax.

Let the lees or bottoms remain a day or two to settle, and then again pour off the liquid, and repeat this until the whole is stored.

This is an admirable pickle, and a truly valuable receipt.

PICCALILLI.

Take a closely-grown, sound-hearted white cabbage and cut it in slices across, a sound white beet-root cut in slices, a cauliflower divided into several small branches, a few clear gherkins, and some radish-pods; also kidney or French beans. Lay them in a sieve with two or three handfuls of common salt scattered over them, and let them be exposed to the sun or placed before a fire four days. When you think all the water is extracted from them, put them into a large pan of stone-ware (I object to glazed vessels for these processes), mixing them well and scattering plenty of good sound mustard seed amongst them as you go on. Then, to each gallon of best vinegar, add

Garlic, peeled and sliced	-	‒ 3 oz.
Turmeric	- -	‒ 1½ oz.

Boil these, and skim them well, and pour the liquor while hot over the vegetables, and let them lie ten days, at least, with strong paper tied over them, near a fire, until they have become a fine yellow colour, and have imbibed a fair quantity of the vinegar. Make then a pickle of the following ingredients : —

Best white wine vinegar	-	- 3 quarts.
White pepper -	-	-	- $1\frac{1}{2}$ oz.
Mace -	-	-	- $1\frac{1}{2}$ oz.
Long pepper -	-	-	- $\frac{1}{2}$ oz.
Nutmeg -	-	-	- $\frac{1}{2}$ oz.
Cloves -	-	-	- $\frac{1}{2}$ oz.

Let them boil ten minutes, and skim them well, and pour all over the pickles. Tie up the jar with bladder and leather.

ASPARAGUS.

Choose the largest asparagus; cut off the white ends so far as you think they would be tough, and lay the green parts in cold water, in which they must be carefully washed, then

taken out, and put in fresh cold water, where
they must remain three hours. Put into a stew-
pan some cold spring water and a small quantity of salt, and when it has boiled take it off
the fire, skim it, and lay in the asparagus heads
with caution or you will break them. Let
them be just scalded (one minute will suffice)
on the fire, and with an egg-slice take them out
and lay them between cloths to cool. Put
them in jars, and make the following pickle : —

Best white wine vinegar - .	- 1 gallon.
Bay-salt - - -	- 1 oz.
Nutmeg - - -	- 1 oz.
Mace - - - -	- $\frac{1}{4}$ oz.
White pepper - - -	- $\frac{1}{2}$ oz.

Let it boil ten minutes, skim it, and pour it
over the asparagus while hot. Tie doubled
linen over the jars, and let them stand six days;
then boil up the pickle again, and pour it over
a second time. When cold, tie your jars over
with bladder and leather.

NASTURTIUMS.

These should be gathered within a week after the blossoms have fallen off. Take a gallon of them, and throw them into a pail of salt and water, cold, in which you must keep them, changing the water three times at least, three days and nights, then lay them in a sieve to drain, and rub them perfectly dry between cloths. Then take

White wine vinegar -	-	- 1 gallon.
Mace -	-	-	- 1 oz.
Nutmeg -	-	-	- 1 oz.
White pepper-corns -	-	- 2 oz.
4 shalots, sliced.			
Common salt	-	-	- 4 oz.

Boil them ten minutes, skim them well, and when nearly cold, pour the whole over the fruit placed in jars, and tie them close.

GREEN SAMPHIRE.

Pick out the refuse from a peck of fine clear green samphire, and let it lie with plenty of salt scattered over and amongst it in an earthern pan two days and nights; then put it in a clean pan with as much water as will cover it, and throw in a handful of salt; set it on the fire to simmer one minute (not more), and add one quart of best vinegar. Let it steam over the fire until it is crisp and of a fine green colour; then take it off immediately, put it in a jar, and when cold tie bladder and leather over it. It will be fit for use in a month.

BARBERRIES.

Take four quarts of barberries when not quite ripe, pick out all the sticks and collect the finest sprigs, which should be tied together in bunches, as they may be wanted for garnishing. Wash them all in salt and water carefully, and set them in a sieve to drain. Place the bunches and the loose ones in separate jars, and pour a pickle of two pounds of common salt mixed with one gallon of water over them, filling the jars

to the brim; skim this pickle well for four or
five days, or as long as any scum rises on it;
then pour off the liquor, and fill the jars again
with new pickle of similar strength, and tie
them closely down for the store-room.   Their
own acidity renders vinegar unnecessary.

WALNUTS PICKLED GREEN.

Take fifty large walnuts gathered before the
shell is hard, and folding them separately in
vine-leaves, place them in a jar amidst plenty
more leaves, so that they do not touch each
other, and fill up so as to cover them with the
best pale vinegar you can procure, and tie
them down closely that the air may be excluded.   Let them stand twenty days, then
pour off the vinegar and wrap the fruit again
in fresh leaves, and fill up the jar again with
fresh pale vinegar, allowing them to stand
fourteen days longer.   Then take off the leaves,
put them in a jar, and make a pickle of white

wine vinegar and salt that will float an egg, in which infuse

Mace	-	-	-	-	- $\frac{1}{4}$ oz.
Cloves	-	-	-	-	- $\frac{1}{2}$ oz.
Nutmeg	-	-	-	-	- $\frac{1}{2}$ oz.

2 heads of garlic, peeled and sliced.

Let it simmer fifteen minutes, and pour it hot over the walnuts; then tie them close with bladder and leather.

WALNUTS PICKLED WHITE.

Choose the largest walnuts for this purpose, and pare them nicely all round until the white or kernel is seen in all parts; put them as you proceed into a brine made with one pound of salt to a gallon of water, and weigh them down so that they are completely immersed, and let them lie so five hours. Then put them into a pan of clear water over the fire, and let them simmer (not boil) for ten minutes. Next throw them into a pan of cold water with a handful of salt, take them out and put them into a pickle of two pounds of salt to the gallon of water, and let them be kept well under for twenty minutes, or they may suffer in colour. Take them out quickly, and lay them between two soft cloths to dry; next wipe each nut gently with soft old linen, and put them into clean dry jars, mixing mace, cloves, and whole pepper, and scattering it equally amongst them as you proceed. Fill up the jars with the best white wine vinegar, then lay strong paper in, and pour melted mutton suet over all. Tie them close.

CAULIFLOWERS.

Choose the whitest and closest grown, and separating them into bunches, lay them on dishes, and strew salt equally all over them; so let them remain three days and nights. Then place them carefully in jars, and pour boiling water over them; tie them close from the air, and let them stand twelve hours; then take them out to dry on a sieve, after which you may put them in your jars or glasses, and

fill up with best white wine vinegar, and tie
bladder and leather over them.

MUSHROOMS PICKLED WHITE.

Take the smallest and roundest button mushrooms, throw them into cold water, and rub
each separately with a piece of soft woollen
cloth dipped in salt to clean them thoroughly.
Put them again, as you proceed, into fresh cold
water, and finally into a pan with a handful of
table salt scattered over them, and put them
over a moderate fire, covering them close that
the steam may not escape, ten minutes, or until
they are thoroughly hot and the water is drawn
well out of them. Pour them then on a sieve,
from whence take them quickly. Dry them well
between two cloths, and let them remain
covered up from the air till they are cold.
Then put them in clean dry glass bottles with
a little mace, and fill them up with distilled or
white wine vinegar, adding to each bottle a
teaspoonful of salad oil ; cork and seal them up

so that the air may be excluded, and they will be excellent in a month.

MUSHROOMS PICKLED BROWN.

Wash two quarts of small mushrooms in salt and water with a flannel thoroughly, and lay them in a pan with common vinegar. Chop three anchovies very small with four shalots peeled, a little mace, cloves, and sliced ginger, with a little cayenne; put these and the mushrooms into a saucepan, with as much vinegar as will just cover them, over a slow fire, and let them simmer until they begin to shrivel. Take them up, and, when cold, put them into bottles, dividing the spices equally, and filling up with the vinegar. Cork and seal them well.

GHERKINS.

Immerse a quarter of a thousand gherkins in a pickle of two and a half pounds of common salt to one gallon of water, and let them

I

lie three hours therein. Put them in a sieve to drain, wipe them separately, and place them in a jar. Prepare a pickle thus,—

Best white wine vinegar	-	- 1 gallon.
Common salt	-	-	- 6 oz.
Allspice	-	-	- 1 oz.
Mustard seed	-	-	- 1 oz.
Cloves	-	-	- $\frac{1}{2}$ oz.
Mace	-	-	- $\frac{1}{2}$ oz.

1 nutmeg, sliced.
1 stick of horseradish, sliced.

Boil it twelve minutes, and skim it well, and pour it when cold over the gherkins, and let them stand twenty hours covered up close; then put them altogether into a pan over the fire, and let them simmer only until they attain a nice green colour; put them into jars, and pour the liquor and spices over them, and tie closely with bladder and leather.

RED CABBAGE.

Take a fine large closely grown cabbage, strip the outside leaves off, cut it across in rather thin slices, and lay them on a dish, scattering salt over them. Cover them with a cloth, and let them lie twenty hours. Next drain the cabbage on a sieve, and put it in a clean jar with allspice, whole pepper, and a little ginger sliced; pour cold white wine vinegar over it to cover it well, and tie closely from the air. The jar should be filled completely. This simple receipt produces the very best flavoured, and most beautifully coloured, cabbage I ever saw and tasted.

SILVER ONIONS.

Procure the smallest clear onions, and after peeling, immerse them in cold salt and water, and let them lie so for ten days, changing the pickle daily. Drain them on a sieve, and, putting them into a jar, pour a newly-made brine of salt and water boiling hot over them, and let them stand closely covered, until cold. Repeat the scalding with new pickle, and, when cold and well drained, put them in bottles or jars, with a slice or two of the best ginger, a blade of mace, and a bay leaf; fill up with distilled vinegar, and be sure to add sweet salad oil to float on the top; then tie close, and, if bottled, cork and seal down for store.

RED CURRANTS.

Gather currants for pickling just before they become fully red; pick out the best bunches, and the soundest of the single ones, and mix with the remainder —

White wine vinegar -	-	- 1 quart.
Loaf sugar -	-	-	- 1 lb.
Table salt -	-	-	- $\frac{1}{4}$ lb.

Boil these gently until the vinegar partakes fairly of the colour of the currants. Skim it well, and let it get cold, strain it through a thick cloth, and afterwards squeeze it well to get all the colour you can. Boil it again, and skim it till clear. Put your bunches and sound fruit into jars and glasses, and pour the liquor hot over them so as to thoroughly cover the currants. You may then tie paper, bladder, and leather closely over.

BEET ROOTS.

Select for pickling, roots of blood-red colour; wash them well, boil them until tender, then peel them quite clear and cut them across in slices not too thin, from which you may make many different fancy shapes. Put them carefully into jars with a little mace, pepper-corns, cloves, horseradish, table salt, and sliced ginger, and fill up with the best vinegar. Tie the jars close with bladder.

GREEN PARSLEY.

Gather as much green, curled parsley as will serve for a year; pick it well and get thence the greatest number of sightly sprigs or branches; throw these into salt and water strong enough to bear an egg, and let them remain one week; then drain them on a sieve, and put them into a fresh pickle of similar strength for a week longer.   Drain them again, and put them in a pan of cold pump water for forty-eight hours, changing the water three times a day.   Then scald them till they become green, dry them well between cloths, and take

White wine vinegar -   -   - 1 quart.
Four blades mace.
One nutmeg, sliced.
Two shalots, peeled and sliced.
One stick of horseradish, sliced.

Boil these twelve minutes, and skim the pickle well.   Put the parsley in jars, and pour the pickle over it when cold, and tie close.

PICKLED CELERY.

Take the white part only of some fine fresh roots of celery, wash, and then wipe them dry. Prepare sufficient pickle to cover them, with an ounce and a quarter of salt, half an ounce of ginger, and as much of white pepper-corns to each quart of vinegar.   When it boils throw in the celery, and when it has boiled two minutes lift it into dry stone jars, and pour the pickle on it; or turn it out, let it cool, and then put it into bottles. It will remain good for a long time, and the vinegar will be found very useful as a dressing to salads when the celery is out of season. If wanted tender at once it must be longer boiled. A very few small button-onions, nicely peeled, may be thrown into the vinegar with it when they are liked. The celery should be cut into short lengths.

TO PICKLE MUSHROOMS,

FOR SAUCE, PIES, ETC. (AN EXCELLENT RECEIPT).

Take a quart of fresh mushroom-buttons — measured after the stalks have been cut closely off; — clean them with a bit of slightly moistened flannel and some fine salt; spread them on a dish, and strew amongst them a small teaspoonful more of salt. Turn them into a very clean broad saucepan, with half a dozen small blades of mace, and about twenty white pepper-corns, and let them simmer until they have absorbed all their own juice; then pour to them a couple of glasses of good white wine, shake the pan round, give them a minute's boil, and add a pint and a half of the best pale vinegar. Boil the mushrooms gently for ten minutes, or rather more, should they be large; put them into very dry bottles or small stone jars, set them in a dry place, and, when they are quite cold, cork them down, and tie bladder over the corks. They make a delicious pickle, and a good sauce, also, for boiled fowls, &c., if drained from the vinegar, and heated in thickened white gravy; they may likewise be added to veal and other pies with advantage. They are very good, even without the wine, but better with it. Sherry or Madeira should be used for them, and the quantity may be doubled with excellent effect, when expense is not an object.

LEMON MANGOES.

Take some fine sound lemons, with rather thick rinds, and cut from the blossom end of each a round, something larger than a shilling; scoop out the insides entirely, rinse them with cold water, to clear them from the loose pulp, and throw them into plenty of brine, made with four ounces of salt to the quart of water. Stir them frequently, change the brine in three days, and let them remain three more; then drain them well, and fill them with bruised mustard seed, and young, finely scraped horse-radish, in about equal proportion, a little ginger sliced thin, and (when the flavour is not objected to), two or three small shalots, or a little garlic; or substitute mustard-seed and small chilies for all the other ingredients. Sew on the parts which have been cut out, lay the lemons closely in a stone jar, and pour boiling on them a pickle made with their own juice, and a large salt-spoonful of salt, half an ounce each of ginger and of white pepper-corns, and a blade or two of mace, to every quart of vinegar. The juice of the fruit should, in the first instance, be pressed from the pulp and strained, and boiled up with sufficient of the vinegar and spice to keep it until the lemons are ready for the pickle. If wanted quickly for eating, set the jar of lemons into a cool oven for one night, to soften them; otherwise, let them stand five or six months.

COMMON SWEET PICKLE OF MELON.

Any well-flavoured melon, taken within two or three days of being quite ripe, will serve for this pickle, which, though a foreign preparation, is much liked by many persons. Pare off all the hard rind of the fruit, scoop out the seeds, and cut it in slices an inch thick; lay it into cold vinegar, which should cover it well, and let it remain a fortnight; then simmer it in fresh vinegar (or in the same, if the flavour be not disliked) until it is tender; drain it well upon a sieve, and, when nearly cold, lay it into jars or glasses, and pour in sufficient pickle to rise an inch above it, made with a pound and two ounces of coarse brown sugar, twenty cloves, and half a drachm of cinnamon in blades, to each pint of vinegar, boiled together' for ten minutes: this may be added to the melon when just warm, but not scalding. It will soon be ready for eating, and is served with stewed and roast beef or mutton: it may also be eaten with pork.

ELDER FLOWER VINEGAR.

To a peck of fresh elder flowers, after they have been divested of all the stalks, put two gallons of white wine vinegar. Set them in a stone jar in the sun fourteen days, and then filter the vinegar through a new flannel bag, and pour it into small clean glass bottles, which must be well corked and sealed.

TARRAGON VINEGAR.

Gather the leaves of Tarragon just before it blossoms, put one pound of them to three quarts of the best white wine vinegar in a stone jar, and let them infuse in it sixteen days. Then drain it from them, and strain it through a flannel bag; add for every two gallons a quarter of an ounce of isinglass dissolved in Sherry wine, and let it be well shaken in a large stone bottle two days; leave it one month to fine, and then draw it off into clean, dry glass bottles, which you will cork and seal up securely.

WHITE GOOSEBERRY VINEGAR.

Take the lightest coloured fruit you can get, when fully ripe, and mash it well with some convenient wooden instrument, a large mallet, or a potato-beetle, for example. To every peck of fruit put two gallons of water, stir them well together for one hour, then let them ferment three weeks, and repeat the stirring daily. Then strain the liquor off, and add for every gallon —

Loaf sugar	-	- 1 lb
Fresh barm or yeast	-	- 1 table spoonful.
Treacle	-	- 1 ditto.

Let it work three days at least, when you may put it into a sweet barrel of appropriate size, and stop it down for twelve months, after which you may bottle it.

N. B. This vinegar will be superior to any white wine vinegar, and as such will be most serviceable in all large domestic establishments. Vinegars should be most especially made at home.

BEST COMMON VINEGAR.

To every gallon of river water add one pound of strong moist sugar, and let it boil ten minutes. Cease not to skim it as long as there is occasion, pour it into a large sweet tub, and, when milk-warm, work it with barm or yeast twenty-four hours, and set in the sunshine, or by the kitchen fire, not too close; when ready, bottle it off into clean stone bottles, and cork them well.

WALNUT CATSUP.

When walnuts are full ripe and ready for eating, take the green outside shells, put them into a jar with as much strong vinegar (cold) as will perfectly cover them, and tie them up securely for twelve months. Then strain them and press the juice out through a strong sieve, and for every gallon of liquor take —

Anchovies, chopped small	-	- 6 oz.
Three heads garlic, peeled.		
Jamaica pepper	-	-	- 1 oz.
Cloves	-	-	-	- 1 oz.
Mace -	-	-	-	- $\frac{3}{4}$ oz.
Black pepper -	-	-	- 1 oz.
Ginger, sliced -	-	-	- 1 oz.
Port wine lees	-	-	- 1 quart.

Let the catsup boil up, and then simmer ten minutes, skim it well, and put it away for twenty-four hours; then boil it until reduced one half.

When cold, you must bottle it for store, and cork and wax it well. It is an excellent catsup, and most useful; and, even when seven years old, is far superior to any I ever met with.

MUSHROOM CATSUP.

Crush the largest and blackest mushrooms you can get, and add to every peck one handful of table salt scattered amongst and over them, and let them lie twenty-four hours. Then put altogether in a deep jar into a moderate oven, and let them stew six hours; then, when cool, strain them well, and boil up the liquor with the following spices —

To each gallon of liquor : —

Mace - - - -	- $\frac{1}{2}$ oz.
Ginger - - - -	- 1 oz.
Jamaica pepper - - -	- 1 oz.
Black pepper-corns - -	- 1 oz.
Cloves - - - -	- 1 oz.
Table salt - - -	- 8 oz.

Let it boil very slowly until it is reduced to half its original quantity. When cold, bottle it off in small bottles, and seal carefully.

TO PREPARE SYRUP FOR PRESERVING FRUIT.

The very best sugar, which will require no clarifying, should be used for this purpose; but, when it is of inferior quality, it must be prepared as follows:—To clarify six pounds of sugar, break it into large lumps, put it into a preserving pan, and pour to it five pints of cold spring water; in another pint beat lightly up the white of one small egg, but do not froth it very much; add it to the sugar, and give it a stir to mix it well with the whole. Set the pan over a gentle fire when the sugar is nearly dissolved, and let the scum rise without being disturbed; when the syrup has boiled five minutes, take it from the fire, let it stand a couple of minutes, and then skim it very clean; let it boil again, then throw in half a cup of cold water, which will bring the remainder of the scum to the surface; skim it until it is perfectly clear, strain it through a thin cloth, and it will be ready for use, or for further boiling.

All unripe fruit must be rendered quite tender by gentle scalding, before it is put into syrup, or it will not imbibe the sugar; and the syrup must be *thin* when it is first added to it, and be thickened afterwards by frequent boiling, or with additional sugar; or the fruit will shrivel instead of becoming plump and clear. A pound of sugar boiled for ten minutes in a pint of water will make a very light syrup; but it will gradually thicken if rapidly boiled in an uncovered pan.   Two pounds of sugar to the pint of water will become thick with little more than half an hour's boiling, or with three or four separate boilings of eight or ten minutes each; if too much reduced it will candy instead of remaining liquid.

LEMONS PRESERVED.

Take a dozen fine lemons, pare the yellow rind off very thin, cut out a piece of the rind at

K

the blossom end, and remove the pulps and pips ;
rub the lemons well all over with fine salt, and
lay them quickly in cold water, and let them
remain five or six days totally immersed;
then boil them in new salt and water twenty
minutes. You should prepare next a syrup of
one pound of loaf sugar to one quart of water
well skimmed, into which put the lemons, and
boil them five or six minutes each for four days
successively; then place them in a jar, and let
them stand six weeks, but they must be perfectly covered by the syrup. After the spe-
cified time, make a thick fine clear syrup of
the best refined sugar and water, put the
lemons into it, and boil them very gently
ten minutes; then set them aside, and after
twenty hours boil them again at short intervals
until they look plump and clear. Then lay them
into jars or glasses, and pour the syrup over
them cold; cover them with brandy paper, and
tie bladder and leather over all.

PEACHES AND NECTARINES.

Select the largest and freshest plums before they are too ripe, rub off the down from them with a piece of old linen cloth, and divide the skin at the seam with the point of a penknife. Immerse them in French brandy in a clean jar, and having tied them down with bladder, let them stand eight or nine days. Then take them out, and have ready a fine clear syrup, into which put and boil them, until they appear beautifully bright. Take the fruit out, place it in glasses, and pour the syrup upon it when it is nearly cold. Lay brandy paper over, and paste writing paper, or tie bladder closely over the tops of the glasses.

GREEN GAGE PLUMS.

The plums for preserving should be gathered just before they are ripe, choosing the largest, free from specks. Lay plenty of vine leaves in the bottom of a pan, and the fruit in layers with leaves between, and covering them well at the top; then fill up with water, and let them get thoroughly hot on a moderate fire; skim them well, and put them in a sieve to cool; after which peel them, and as you proceed put them again into the water in which they were boiled, with fresh layers of leaves, and let them boil three minutes, keeping the steam in as much as possible; let them remain at a moderate distance from the fire, six or seven hours, until they become green; this done, put them into a sieve to drain, and then boil them up in a good clear syrup once a day for three successive days. Take them out and lay them in glasses or jars, skim the syrup well, and pour it, when nearly cold, over the plums, and put brandy paper over them. Tie close down, and the result will be most satisfactory.

APRICOTS.

Just before they are too ripe take some of
the largest and soundest apricots, pick them
carefully, and push the stones out at the stalk
ends with a blunt piece of wood; weigh the
fruit, and for every pound of apricots allow one
pound of the best loaf sugar, the half of which,
when well beaten to powder and sifted, you
must strew over the fruit, and let them lie
twenty-four hours. Boil them gently up, and
when they have become cold repeat the boiling
five or six times, at intervals of four or five
hours; by which means they will have become
clear and bright. Take them out, and when you
have made a good thick clear syrup, boil the
apricots up in it five minutes, skimming it well.
You may then put them in glasses or jars, and
pour the syrup over them, using brandy paper
and bladder.

GRAPES.

Take the grapes when just ripe, pick them from the stalks singly, and put them into a pan with powdered loaf sugar strewed slightly between them: before you put them on the fire bruise the fruit a little, and let them simmer until the seeds rise to the top. These must be skimmed off as long as any appear. When they are sufficiently done take them off the fire and pour them on to a fine sieve, placed over a clean pan to receive the juice. Pick out of the fruit any seeds that you may find, and if the preserve is too tart add more powdered sugar to the syrup, which must be boiled up again and skimmed well. Lay the fruit in glasses or jars, and pour the syrup upon it, nearly filling them to the top: cover them, when cold, with brandy paper and bladder.

PRESERVED DAMSONS.

Take the finest prune damsons, not too ripe, cut them open lengthways and take out the stones; put them into a pan with as much water as will cover them, and let them boil for ten minutes; then pour them on to a sieve, and wipe them separately. Allow for each pound of fruit one pound of the best loaf sugar; the half of which, when sifted fine, you must strew over the damsons laid upon large dishes; put the other half of the sugar to the liquor in which the fruit was boiled, and setting it on the fire, let it boil up; then skim it well, and let it simmer ten minutes; put in the fruit and boil it well up, take it off and let it stand, closely covered, twenty minutes; put it again to simmer half an hour, and let it stand till next day, when you will boil it again until it is tender; put the damsons into a sieve and boil the jelly by itself one hour: you may then put the fruit into jars and pots, and pour the jelly over it hot.

When cold, put brandy paper over, and melted mutton suet above that, and tie bladder over the jars.

RED CURRANTS IN BUNCHES.

Gather the finest bunches on a dry warm day, and having brushed off the dust and insects with a feather, tie them to spills of wood six inches long ; put their weight of best loaf sugar into a pan with as much water as will dissolve it and boil it five minutes, skimming it well. Take the pan off the fire and lay in it the sticks with care, and let the fruit boil up ten minutes slowly. Take off the pan, and when cool, disengage the bunches and place them in glasses or pots. Add to the syrup half a pint of good currant jelly of the same colour as the fruit, boil it up, skimming it well till quite clear, and pour it, when cool, over the fruit, covering it well. When cold, put brandy paper over, and paste white paper over the glasses. Set them in a cool, dry room, and they will be excellent in three months.

MORELLO CHERRIES.

The cherries must be sound, thoroughly ripe, and carefully picked from the stalks, and, being wiped separately, must be pricked each four or five times with a small needle. Then, allowing one pound and a half of best loaf sugar to each pound of fruit, strew one half of it, well pounded and sifted, over the cherries on a clean dry dish; so let them remain eighteen hours. Then take as much red currant juice as will dissolve the remaining half of the sugar, and put it into a pan over a moderate fire, and let it boil ten minutes; skim it well, put in the cherries with their sugar, and let all simmer five minutes, not allowing them to boil. Then take out the fruit, and put it in glasses; boil up the syrup until it is thick, and pour it cool over the cherries. Put brandy paper on them, and paste paper over the glasses.

CUCUMBERS.

Procure twenty of the largest and greenest cucumbers, free from seeds and spots; cut them in pieces, take out the soft part, and put them in a jar, with strong salt and water to cover them, and set them in a warm place until they become yellow. Wash them well, and set them in a pan of water on the fire well covered with cabbage leaves; close the saucepan to keep in the steam, and simmer them till of a fine green colour. If requisite, change the water and leaves, and simmer them again. Then take them out, and put them on a sieve to cool, and put them into cold water two days, changing the water four times. Set four pounds of loaf sugar and one quart of pure water in a pan over the fire; boil and skim it well; then add the rinds of four lemons pared very thin, and three ounces of the best ginger sliced, and boil all together ten minutes. Take it off the fire, and, when cool, put in the cucumbers and boil them until they are quite clear. Should they not appear so, set them aside for forty-eight hours, and repeat the boiling until you succeed to your wishes. Then put the cucumbers in glasses or pots, and pour the syrup over them when cool. Use brandy paper, &c.

BARBERRIES IN BUNCHES.

Procure the largest bunches of fine clear barberries, and having picked off any faulty ones, put them with as much water as will be requisite to make their syrup, into a pan, and boil them until tender. Next strain them through a sieve, and to every pint of their juice add one pound and a half of best loaf sugar; boil and skim this well, and to each pint of the syrup put half a pound of the fruit in bunches, and boil them gently until they become thoroughly bright and clear. When cold, put them in glasses, and pour the syrup over them; apply brandy paper, and paste paper over the glasses.

If you wish to preserve any for tarts, pick them free from stalks, and put them, with their own weight of good sugar, finely powdered, into a jar, which, being tied at the top with bladder, must be put into a saucepan of boiling water on the fire, and kept boiling until the sugar is dissolved and the barberries are tender. Set them aside twenty-four hours, then boil them up again twenty minutes, and when lukewarm dispose of them in pots and glasses, putting brandy paper and bladder over them.

GRAPES PRESERVED WHOLE.

When just ripe lay some fine bunches in a wide jar, and to each pound of fruit allow one ounce of white sugar candy, beaten small, which, as the grapes are laid in, must be scattered equally amongst them. Fill up the jar with Betts's patent brandy, tie it closely over with bladder and leather, and keep it in a dry, airy room.

CURRANTS FOR TARTS.

Gather your fruit in favourable weather, and pick out the best for your preserves. Press the juice out of the refuse currants, and strain it through a hair sieve. Allow one pound of best loaf sugar to each pound of fruit, and make a fine clear syrup of the sugar and currant juice. When it is cold put in your fruit and let it boil until beautifully clear, when it may be put in pots or glasses, and covered with brandy paper, and then with bladder, well cleaned and wiped very dry.

GREEN CODLINS.

Gather them when they have attained the size of a walnut, with a part of the stalk on. Take plenty of vine leaves and lay the codlins in layers, covering them with water; put them on the fire and let them simmer, confining the steam as much as possible, until they are tender, then take them up and lay them in a sieve to cool. Pare them neatly, and put them again into the water they were boiled in when it is quite cold, or you may cause them to crack; put fresh vine leaves over them, and simmer them until they are green, which may be effected sooner by adding a small quantity of alum.

Put them in jars, and pour over them when cold a thick clear syrup; put brandy paper over them, and tie bladder and leather over it, and set them in a dry and cool place for store.

GOLDEN PIPPINS.

Pare one dozen pippins nicely, cut them in quarters, and take way the cores. Boil the rinds of two oranges quite tender, and lay them in a pan of cold water three days. Put these into a pan with as much water as will cover them, and let them boil twenty minutes, and strain the juice through a jelly bag; then pare a dozen more pippins, take out the core at the

stalk ends neatly. Make a fine clear syrup of
two pounds of best loaf sugar and one pint of
water, to which add the apple juice, and when
it is cold put in the pippins, adding the orange
peels cut in thin shreds. Boil all very gently
for ten minutes, take out the pippins, when cool,
put them in jars and pour the syrup over them.
Put brandy paper over them, and bladder again
over that, tied closely. If you choose, you may
melt mutton suet, and pour it upon the brandy
paper.

FINE RHUBARB JAM.

Let the rhubarb be drawn on a dry day;
wipe the stalks clean, but do not wash them,
peel off the skin and coarse fibres, and slice
the stalks thin. To each pound thus prepared allow a pound of sugar in fine powder;
put the fruit in a pan, and strew a quarter of
the sugar amongst and over it; let it stand
until the sugar is dissolved, then boil it slowly
to a smooth pulp; take it from the fire, and

stir in the remainder of the sugar by degrees,
and when it is melted, boil the preserve quickly
until it becomes very thick, and leaves the bottom of the pan visible when stirred. The time
required for this preserve will depend on the
kind of rhubarb used, and the time of year in
which it is made, and will vary from an hour
and a half to two hours and a quarter. The
juice should be slowly drawn from it at first.

ANOTHER RHUBARB JAM.

(MANCHESTER RECEIPT).

Boil gently together for three hours an
equal weight of fine sugar and rhubarb stalks,
with the juice and grated rind of a lemon to
each pound of the fruit. When the true flavour
of the rhubarb is much liked, the lemon-peel
should be omitted. A very good jam may be
made with six ounces less of sugar to the
pound, by boiling the rhubarb gently for an
hour before it is added.

JAM OF MORELLO CHERRIES.

This is a delicious preserve when made with fine ripe morellos. Stone the fruit, weigh it, heat it rather slowly to draw out the juice, then boil it quickly for twenty minutes over a very clear fire ; add thirteen ounces of sugar for each pound of the cherries, and boil the jam from fifteen to twenty minutes longer, being careful to clear off all the scum. The sugar should be of good quality ; it must be beaten to powder, and added gradually to the fruit, and stirred with it, off the fire, until it is dissolved. A larger portion may be used when the morellos are very acid. An equal weight with the cherries will not be too much for some tastes ; but their flavour will be better preserved with less. A few of the kernels, blanched and wiped quite dry, may be added a couple of minutes before the jam is poured out.

RED CURRANT JELLY OF FINE FLAVOUR
MADE WITHOUT BOILING.

The fruit for this jelly, which may be made entirely of red currants, or with equal parts of white and red, should be fine and quite ripe; it should also be gathered when very dry, and used the same day. Pick it from the stalks, and squeeze the juice from it through a thick cloth; make it scalding hot, but do not allow it to boil; pass it through a jelly bag, measure it, and for every pint, exact measure, allow a pound of the best sugar, weighed after it is sifted. Heat the currant-juice as before, but let it not boil; then add the sugar, which should also have been made quite hot, stirring it in quickly, by degrees. Continue to stir it until the whole is dissolved; take off the scum, and pour the jelly into shallow pans. Let it remain uncovered in a dry place, and it will soon become quite firm; it should then be covered with writing paper dipped in spirit or with double tissue paper, which will answer the purpose as well. It will jelly more quickly with a pound and two ounces of sugar to the pint of juice.

RASPBERRY MARMALADE.

Pick some fresh ripe raspberries from the stalks, and simmer them gently about ten minutes, keeping them often stirred. Pour them with their juice into a new or very clean hair sieve, and rub them through it with a wooden spoon, leaving only the seeds behind. Weigh the fruit, and boil it quickly for eight or ten minutes; take the pan from the fire, and stir gradually to it three quarters of a pound of sugar to the pound of pulp. When this is quite dissolved, continue the boiling for another ten minutes; less time will sometimes be sufficient; but the thickness of the preserve, and the manner in which it jellies on the skimmer, will show when it is boiled enough. The raspberries may be rubbed through a sieve without the previous simmering, then mixed with their weight of sugar, and boiled quickly for twenty minutes.

Rich strawberry jam or marmalade is made in precisely the same manner.

BLACK CURRANTS FOR TARTS OR PUDDINGS.

To four pounds of black currants ready stripped from the stalks, allow two pounds and a half of good white sugar coarsely powdered. Put the fruit into a preserving pan, strew two tablespoonfuls of sugar over it, and turn it gently with a wooden spoon until it has boiled five minutes; then mix the remainder of the sugar well with it, off the fire, and boil it quickly for fifteen minutes, being careful to keep it stirred, and to remove the scum as it rises. When the currants are very sweet and rich, eight ounces of the sugar may be omitted. The preserve will keep well covered with brandied paper only, if stored in a quite dry place. It should not be firm like jam except just upon the surface.

BLACK CURRANT MARMALADE.

(GOOD FOR A COUGH.)

Take the currants when they are fully ripe, strip them from the stalks, bruise them a little in the preserving pan, and stew them gently, keeping them turned until they are tender, which they will generally be in from ten to fifteen minutes. Pour off about three parts of the juice, which will make excellent jelly, and rub the remainder with the currants through a sieve. Weigh the pulp, boil it rapidly for a quarter of an hour, or for twenty minutes if there should be a large quantity of it; then, for each pound, stir into it, until dissolved, nine ounces of white sugar rolled or pounded fine; boil the marmalade quickly for ten minutes, stirring it often, and pour it into small pans. If well made it will cut out in firm slices.

TO PRESERVE VEGETABLES GREEN AND FRESH.

French Beans.

Gather on a fine day the youngest and clearest French beans, wipe them well, and put them in a stone jar with layers of table salt between them until it is quite full. Press them closely down, and put a piece of slate on the top of the vegetables with more salt upon that, and tie bladder over. Place them in a dry cellar. When you wish to use them, take some out of the jar (covering the remainder close again), wash them well in cold water, and lay them in fresh cold water twenty-four hours. Then boil them in plenty of water, adding a lump of butter while cooking.

Green Peas.

Choose them young and fine, shell them, and throw them into boiling hot water with a handful of salt, and let them lie six minutes off the fire. Pour them into a cullender, and dry them thoroughly between cloths. Take clean

dry glass jars or bottles, fill them to the neck
with the peas, shaking them down, then pour
melted mutton suet over them, and cork them
up close.

Green Gooseberries.

Put one ounce of roche-alum into a panful of
hot water, and let it boil one minute. Have your
gooseberries ready picked, and with a small
sieve immerse them in the water until you per-
ceive they begin to lose their colour; take them
out quickly; dry them between cloths, and when
cold, put them into dry clean bottles, rejecting
any broken ones. When the water in which
they were steeped is cold, fill the bottles with
it, and put a teaspoonful of salad oil into each.
Cork well and seal them close.

CUCUMBER VINEGAR.
(FOR FISH AND SALADS.)

First wipe, and then slice thin into a jar, some
freshly cut cucumbers, the most free from seeds
that can be had; season the layers with fine salt

and plenty of pepper, and pour boiling to them as much pale vinegar as will cover them entirely. Let them remain a month, or even longer, well secured from the air; then strain the vinegar very clear, put it into clean dry bottles, and cork them closely: a tablespoonful of Chili vinegar to the pint of common, is an improvement for this preparation, and a mild onion or two is sometimes sliced and laid into the jar with the cucumbers.

GOOD CURRIE POWDER.

(EAST INDIAN RECEIPT.)

Coriander seed, pounded and sifted	- 6 ozs.
Turmeric - - -	- 1½ oz.
Cummin seed - - -	- 1½ oz.
Fœnugreek seed - -	- 1½ oz.
Cardamoms - - -	- ½ oz.
Cayenne pepper - -	- 6 drachms.

The seeds should be weighed after they have been well pounded, and passed through a fine sieve. Half an ounce of cloves is sometimes added to the above.

ANOTHER GOOD CURRIE POWDER.

Coriander seed	-	-	- 8 ozs.
Turmeric	-	-	- 4 ozs.
Powdered ginger	-	-	- 2 ozs.
Pounded mace	-	-	- 1 drachm.
Cummin seed	-	-	- 1 oz.
Fœnugreek	-	-	- 2 ozs.
Mushroom powder	-	-	- 1 oz.

THE END.